# PRAYING IN THE PINE STRAW

## THE CAMP-MEETING EXPERIENCE IN ALABAMA

**ROBERT C. MORGAN**

THE UNIVERSITY OF ALABAMA PRESS
Tuscaloosa

The University of Alabama Press
Tuscaloosa, Alabama 35487-0380
uapress.ua.edu



Typeface: Janson Text LT Std

Cover image: stock.adobe.com
Cover design: Sandy Turner Jr.

Cataloging-in-Publication data is available from the Library of Congress.
ISBN: 978-0-8173-2249-6 (cloth)
ISBN: 978-0-8173-6221-8 (paper)
E-ISBN: 978-0-8173-9578-0

# PRAYING IN THE PINE STRAW

For my mother, Barbara, who would have loved the music at camp meeting.

# Contents

# Figures

# Preface

It's a fair question: What do the following pages represent? In attempting to answer that, allow me to cite a couple of stories from 1888, roughly the middle of the era that is under perusal here regarding the camp-meeting phenomenon in Alabama, neither story having anything remotely to do with praying in the pine straw. The stories were about Alabama men in specific Alabama locations, stories carried in Alabama newspapers. Both stories, oddly enough, involved men from Greenville, Alabama, in Butler County, and naturally make me curious about what exactly was going on in that neck of the woods in October 1888. Curiosity, however, is secondary to the lesson I hope the stories provide for understanding the materials herein. In one story, W. D. Newman was visiting relatives near Elba on Haw Ridge in Coffee County, Alabama, when he went wildcat hunting with some young men. They were on the Pea River a few miles from Elba when something dropped out of a tree, covered W. D. Newman's head, cut his cheek, bit off an ear, and nearly sliced his throat. The animal was said to be on the order of a wildcat, but was webbed, like a flying squirrel. Its face was flat, had three-inch teeth, bulging eyes, short but stiff hair, short legs, webbed-feet, and sharp claws. The twenty-six-pound creature, reportedly killed after the attack, was described as a vampire bat-wildcat hybrid. A vampire bat, it was noted, had escaped a circus in that area years before. In the other story, S. B. Brown was on the road between Monterey and Rocky Creek in Butler County and discovered a cave that, unfortunately, he decided to explore. Inside, he was accosted by a monster standing four-and-a-half-feet tall with three-foot-long arms, a head, without benefit of neck, perched on its shoulders, a hairy upper body, a bare lower body, and feet like eagles' claws. And, oh yeah, the face was like a gorilla's! The thing let out a yowl and jumped on S. B. Brown, and, had it not been for a couple of men passing by who heard the commotion, the demon would have killed Mr. Brown. Yes, *demon!* The thing ripped Brown's clothing to shreds and cut him up good and proper, enough to require a doctor's care. A posse returned to the cave and dispatched the demon-thing and displayed the odd creature at a local gin house.

The point to be made here is that what follows concerning the camp meeting in Alabama is best described in terms of those creatures that allegedly attacked the Greenville men in 1888. It's kind of a hybrid-thing I'm putting forth, or so I'm led to understand by those in the know; it's neither fish nor fowl; it's history but personal reminiscence, a meditation, a memoir. Whatever this hybrid is, it's my take on the phenomenon of the camp meeting, shooting for objectivity, yet with personal elements interspersed. But unlike in 1888, when the offbeat hybrid-creature stories appeared and some state newspapers concluded that the stories of the wildcat-vampire and cave-demon likely were the result of "blind tigers," places that sold illegal alcohol (W. D. Newman was apparently at home on Persimmon Creek when he was said to be gushing blood on Haw Ridge from a strange animal attack), I swear I'm undertaking the following story soberly and totally sober. As one of the newspapers that questioned the wildcat-vampire story pointed out, there was likely plenty of alcohol available to preserve the strange creature. Here, the only traces of alcohol involved are those reported back in the day at Alabama camp-meeting sites. The only license I take is one of birthright, and that involves something cherished by us Alabama natives, namely, the right of *narrative.* It's a right so tradition-bound and venerated that sometimes we choose a made-up narrative to follow rather than what history records. I've tried not to do that.

# PRAYING IN THE PINE STRAW

# Introduction

## Ichabod in the Pulpit

Years ago, as a young man, I used to dove hunt with a friend in the vicinity of Dixons Mill in neighboring Marengo County, Alabama; that's the southwest corner of the state. Back then, the small, unincorporated community, sometimes spelled "Dixon's Mill" or "Dixon's Mills," had one claim to fame as far as I knew: it was as the site of a sometime large religious gathering. It was all pretty murky to me, that event that put Dixons Mill on the map when religious fervor arose at set times on the calendar. I didn't know anything about the "camp meeting," or its role in American history, and, even if I had, I feel certain it wouldn't have interested me at that stage of life the way hunkering down on a fence row on a crisp fall Saturday did and listening on a crackling transistor radio to John Forney broadcast another University of Alabama football game, all the while keeping an eye on the sky for a slashing, darting dove.

Actually, the camp meeting could be as exciting as a dove hunt and just as unpredictable; it could be as dangerous as it was uplifting and, especially unsettling, way too *entertaining* for some campers. Sure, you expected birdshot to rain down on your head occasionally in a dove field, but when heaven and earth got together at a camp meeting, well, you never knew where the stinging pellets might fall or where they were coming from or whom they might hit. "In the world but not of it." That was an oft-repeated maxim concerning the church and Christians when I was a boy. I'll not be brazen here and get a religious scrap started by denying that old slogan; rather, in the spirit of fellowship, I'll simply say the camp meeting offered historical proof that the world is a hard place to flee, no matter how deep into the woods one goes, even kneeling on pine straw at nature's altar. People got peppered from above and below, stung, as it were, by things that occurred when people turned aside to commune with God and each other. See, the world still called the shots by and large, especially when America was young and campers were pioneers. The camp-meeting date was usually set after crops were gathered. Weather impacted the prospects for a camp meeting the way it did crops in the field, affecting whether there would be a bounty of souls harvested or not. Worldly contrivances, such as the railroad and automobile, made it possible for more people to camp but, then, quickly, became reasons to don sackcloth and ashes as innovations that took Americans away from camping and God. Time ultimately took its toll on the camp meeting; the irresistible passing of time essentially resulted in the passing of the encampments themselves. Into the woods or fields or groves of the camp meeting went human nature too, the very thing the camp meeting was trying to rectify religiously, but it too proved as intractable as time. The "fallen" nature of humans, with their skewed convictions about everything under the sun—their politics, their appetites, their devotion to American capitalism—made the camp meeting a historical flare that burned out almost immediately; a holy ghost that would be pursued for generations by those who thought lightning could be trapped in a bottle twice. It never was, and it probably couldn't be. Still, the quest by some for old-timey religion lives on.

Certainly, the heyday of the camp meeting was long past by the time I was hunting in Dixons Mill. The Marengo Union Camp Meeting as it was called came to be in the early years of the twentieth century, long after the crowning point of the camp-meeting phenomenon. Not even marquee preachers, such as Bob Jones and Gypsy Smith, who preached at camp meetings in Dixons Mill could resurrect what had occurred a hundred years before. The best they could do was an echo of the past, when America was young and giving birth to a peculiar religious experience. What follows in these pages is like birdshot. It's a single pellet—a BB—separated from the "load" with specificity for Alabama. It's well-intentioned in that it hopes to be an accurate historical portrayal of the camp-meeting experience in Alabama. It's not meant to be critical or negative, but as objective as humanly possible. The narrative is, however, about *uneasiness* in the camp-meeting experience, meaning occurrences that took place in real time didn't get the same attention as the flowery orations and reminiscences about salvation and repentance and godly men and women seeking a Heavenly Zion in some woodland bower. If what follows comes off as uncharitable and stings the cheek like a shotgun pellet, so be it. Just remember that a famous religionist (St. Paul) once said that charity "rejoiceth in the truth." That said, this writer offers what follows in the certitude that knowledge "shall vanish away" (St. Paul again), which, regretfully, seems even more of a certainty today. Still, it is tissue-like knowledge, feathery in nature as it may be, that quickens the pages that follow. Referring to St. Paul yet again, if I be deemed a "child" hunkered down on that fencerow in Marengo County, eyeing the sky for dove, I eventually "put away childish things" (caveat: without forsaking the love of bird hunting) and became a "man." In that latter transformation I became a southern religionist, and, along the way, the Marengo Union Camp Meeting eventually became of interest to me the way Marengo County dove did in my salad days.

Along the way, I learned that, broadly speaking, there's an extreme element historically in southern religion. Sure, there's a snake-handling component practiced by a small group that has been known to drink poison to show their faith, but that community is minuscule. I've never seen a rattlesnake or copperhead introduced into a church service, certainly not poison, although a few dishes occasionally made their way to the table at dinners-on-the-ground that came close. No, the extreme element I'm referring to here in the southern style of religion's DNA comes from revivalism and the old camp meetings. Regarding those influences, I likewise have never seen a believer run around on all fours and bark, but "treeing the devil" was not uncommon at those weeks-long camp meetings on the frontier. Likewise, there was babbling in tongues, swooning, dancing, jerking, and other manifestations of religious ecstasy when the Holy Spirit descended. Now, there were examples of "swooning" and "ecstasy" that occurred apart from the Holy Spirit at camp meetings, and those resulted in more than a few illegitimate children. The camp meeting could occasion a kind of unspoken

Figure 1. One Lucien Pitts from Seale, Alabama, was photographed around 1916 handling a snake. Around that same time a religious cult involving snake handling as witness to one's faith had sprung up in the Sand Mountain–Scottsboro area in the northeastern corner of the state. Alabama Department of Archives and History.

Old Testament "be fruitful and multiply" culture; this was a "spiritual" hazard that wasn't part of the accepted camp-meeting agenda, so it didn't get that much play in religious histories. Yet, it was bound to happen when a bunch of socially isolated people on the frontier came together looking for consolation, be it spiritual or otherwise. It was just one of those *uneasy* aspects of camping for Jesus. Likewise, I've never seen anybody dance a holy jig in church, bellow out a holy laugh, or get healed. I've never even heard an unknown tongue in church.

Still, I knew well the leaven that permeated the unusual manifestation that was the camp meeting of the nineteenth and early twentieth centuries. I recall one gospel fast-gun, a preacher from Mobile, who came to my home church as a visiting evangelist during a week of revival services. He was tall and rangy, a cross between Jack Wilson, the gunslinger in *Shane*, and Ichabod Crane in "The Legend of Sleepy Hollow." That guy's southern drawl of the gospel had a way of suspending us over the fires of hell indefinitely, until we could smell sulfur in our nostrils and feel the waves of hellfire rising out of the pit. It—he!—made you want to bolt from the packed house to gasp for air. Everything was word-stretched, delivered in syllables that didn't exist, and included descriptive overkill regarding the end times, Jesus' return (always just around the corner!), Rapture, Antichrist, and other apocalyptic strands that left us weak as water and trembling. It was as gut wrenching as I imagine hefting religious rattlesnakes to be! Throw in an unhealthy dollop of predestination, and, well, you could be assured of staring at the ceiling as you tried to sleep after hearing God's rail-like messenger, he the flesh and bones incarnation of God's wrath, say 1) your eternal fate was sealed one way or another—destination heaven, destination hell—by the Almighty before you were born, but 2) you needed to be saved. Such ambiguity was part of God's mysteries and impossible to unravel, much like shaking the Reverend Ichabod's hand each night and thanking him for scaring hell out of us, making us nearly swoon with religious terror, creating uncertainly regarding where we would spend eternity, and leading some to repeat the rite of baptism—a kind of insurance policy against the "sinners in the hands of an angry God" theme with which we were constantly bombarded. God was always angry, even when loving us! The success of a revival was thus measured in anxious sweat by the congregants, sleeplessness, tears, and the sneaky suspicion that you'd never measure up—you couldn't—when Jesus cleaved the heavens. See, the standard of righteousness to be aspired to wasn't from Jesus or from anything set forth in the Bible as a whole. No, we wanted to achieve the level of *certainty* exhibited by God's enforcers, the grim spiritual taskmasters that preached to us without a scintilla of doubt in what they said or believed. That's what made a week of revival services as perilous as a fistful of copperheads; the nightly measuring of oneself against the straight shooter in the pulpit. That was a relic that came through the camp meeting, the business of getting the best no-nonsense preacher to double-down at the camp meeting; the one who could open the flood gates of repentance, leave sinners helpless or jerking or barking—that way the Holy Spirit could come in unimpeded and "slay" them. Get the right man, or men, to preach. Get the man who could raise the tally of the heaven-bound and had a reputation for saving hardscrabble pioneer souls. Getting this man made all the difference between a successful camp meeting and a so-so one. It was a powder-keg, the camp meeting was, and a spark could set the whole thing off. That's why the right camp-meeting preacher cut a wide swath and was so much in demand at altars and tabernacles in the pine straw. He was "on fire" for the Almighty—a firebrand, a flamethrower.

I knew about the spiritual combustibility firsthand. Once, as the pastor of a Southern Baptist church, I saw firsthand how the atmosphere of a revival service was altered by a visiting youth choir that introduced elements into the service that weren't the norm in our rather sedate congregation. The charismatic-leaning youth group introduced a momentary "spirit" that was contagious, and it spread like wildfire and resulted in an altered state of consciousness for those present. I was there and saw it (and experienced it) myself. Nobody treed the devil or fell into a fit of holy laughter, but a change occurred that was *felt.* It can happen at a funeral, in situations where the homiletic send-off becomes so emotional and the singing so primitive, that a kind of *suspension* of reality takes place. It's most discernible in the one receiving the send-off; how the description of the pilgrim going home bears little resemblance to the pilgrim of the earthly way, though both were the same person. Seriously, don't underestimate what an accordion can do at a funeral!

Vestiges from the camp-meeting era continue to live on in southern religious expressions in innumerable ways, passed down as part of our spiritual heritage. Likewise, those become part of the cultural fabric of Alabama in ways too numerous to mention here and outside the scope of this study. Consider just one: the state's proclivity for the governorship to be in the hands of a "Christian." In the modern era alone, Alabama has elected a Primitive Baptist preacher (Guy Hunt); a Sunday School teacher and deacon (Robert Bentley); the son of a preacher (W. W. "Plain Bill" Brandon); an anti-evolutionist and an advoctate for the Ten Commandments in the courtroom (Fob James); and a man, according to radical communistfighter Dr. Carl McIntire, deemed the essence of a Bible-believing governor and, according to Jew fighter Gerald L. K. Smith, deemed to be Christlike (George Wallace). Without acknowledging some level of Christian affiliation and/or identity with a Christian body, well, let's just say the keys to the governor's mansion will be out of reach for any politician seeking the state's highest office. What the "Christians" do while in office actually becomes secondary to the fact that, if not having actually knelt at the old brush arbor, they at least voice some affinity for the perception of old-time religion.

Figure 2. Even with the heyday of the camp meeting long past, belief in turning away from the world and worldly activity for spiritual benefit and refreshment was unabated. The spiritual benefit of fresh air was inherent in this woodland sign from the 1950s pointing the way to Camp McDowell, an Episcopal retreat and conference center, in Nauvoo in Walker County. Alabama Department of Archives and History.

Whoa! Hold on! the cry will undoubtedly go up. You can't make a jump like that! Well, call it a "jump" if you like; I call it just one "step"—a "pirouette" if you like—in the holy dance we've been doing since the camp-meeting era; it's just part of the choreography of dancing a holy jig that's become second nature to us. Me, crazy? Well, that's what was said of those who experienced the great camp meeting that became the template for all those that would follow in young America. Those first campers, it was said, were left "insane" and "demented" by too much Holy Spirit, too many visions, too much religious frenzy. Don't kid yourselves: there were dangers in going into the wilderness to encounter the Holy Spirit. I will concede this as far as what lies ahead in these pages. Let's not do something here at the outset that would have been a hindrance to getting to a camp meeting back in days of yore, namely, getting the cart (wagon) before the horse. Let's look back first; then each of us can decide about the camp meeting—whether it's a historical relic, like dinosaur bones, or something we're still beholden to, a *spirit* that grips us down to the present day.

# 1

## "No Doctrine So Humble but It Can Find Supporters; No Prophet So Crazy but He Can Attract Converts"

In 1907, a journalist of the day gave Alabama readers of the *Birmingham News* a history lesson in a sprawling article that was special to the newspaper.[1] The journalist tagged practically every region of the country as contributors to the "increasing number of freak cults" as he put it. According to him, Chicago had a colony of "Gluckites," which included the forty or so followers of Dr. Asher Gluck, a seeker after a perfect world. The only problem was that the *Chicago Tribune* couldn't confirm the existence of the forty since nobody had ever seen them.[2] The three-story building where the Gluckites allegedly lived was described by the *Tribune* as "locked and dreary" and likely occupied by only the good doctor and his wife. The Gluck colony, if indeed there was one apart from Asher Gluck's imagination, was based on separation from the world and a belief that the only way to save the country was to rear perfect children. When Dr. Gluck showed up in New York looking not for converts but clothes—the Gluckite signature dress was brown linen suits—he and his Simple Life Colony in Chicago were identified as "Architects of the New Race," Dr. Gluck being the "Chief Architect."[3] Regarding perfect children, Dr. Gluck, holder of degrees from German and Austrian schools, said this to the New York newspaper: "As their parents we live a perfectly simple life. We are vegetarians. We work eight hours, study eight hours, and sleep eight hours. We slay no living thing; we use no leather, for it is of the hide of a dead creature, and no bristles in brushes for the same reason. We live naturally, wear no underclothes, and our women no corsets, nor do they tie their hair upon their heads. Our apparel is linen entirely, even to the soles of our shoes." Identifying himself as springing from the tribe of Judah, bearded Asher Gluck said this about the Gluckites' not inconsequential goal: "We want a perfect race, and believe that in the perfect child of such parents as we are trying to make will be the immortality of the parents."[4]

Underwear and corsets notwithstanding, Chicago wasn't the only area of the country with a freak cult, according to the journalist. Kansas, Texas, and Ohio all had "incubated" colonies similar to the Gluckites. The Texas version was an attempt to establish an "Adamless Eden." Needless to say, a proposed colony of emancipated women was bound to draw derision and did. "Those thousand Chicago women who intend to establish an Adamless Eden in Texas intend to raise sugar beets, according to the Chicago papers. Adamless Eden women will find Texas better adapted to raising a Cain crop."[5] The brain trust behind Adamless Eden, Mary F. Haydon of Chicago, was a novelist with a background in newspapers and a close friend of Frances Willard, the temperance worker.[6] Plans were for the colony of women to occupy five thousand acres on the Texas Gulf coast where they would "embark in truck farming, fruit raising, beekeeping, dairying, poultry raising, and other kindred farm and ranch pursuits." It wasn't that men or husbands were excluded from the colony; it was just that the women would be in absolute control and "Adam" would be left to do the "distastefull [*sic*] and laborious hard work." A railroad official tasked with getting the women colonists to the proposed site put in his unsolicited two cents regarding the colony, namely, that women in charge of the whole shebang would only result in minding each others' business and "scrapping among themselves" to the point that none would have time to mind their own business. "One thousand self-sustaining women, all by their lonesome, would be a sight to make angels weep and prudent men take to the woods. Individually I believe in women, but collectively—excuse me please. Women are all right in homeopathic doses, but without men to add variety to their daily life, they will get so tired of each others' society they will fight like the 'Kilkenny cats.'" In Irish folklore, the Kilkenny cats fought each other so ferociously that only their tails were left. That was the conclusion of one "Adam" regarding the prospect of a freak colony run solely by women.

"Enthusiastic socialists" in places like New York and New Jersey created a variety of cultic sensations that passed for religion, at least, so said the journalist. Perhaps he was talking about the Adamless Eden Hotel in New York City for one. The Martha Washington started out as a hotel exclusively for women but by 1907, in spite of a "full house and a spotlessness of character that made other hostelries green with envy," was closing its doors.[7] Or take the kind of experiment conducted by Trinity Methodist Church in Trenton, New Jersey, a one-time service where the pastor turned everything over to the "fair sex."[8] Women would do the preaching, lead the choir, conduct the altar call, and pass out the collection plates. No men allowed, at least, that one time. Perhaps the hotel and church in question met the criteria in the day for enthusiastic social experimentation passing for religion.

Anything connected with socialists or socialism was open to broad interpretation and misrepresentation, but not so the strain of cult freakiness ascribed to the South and West. "Holy Rollers" was the name outsiders pelted them with. That's pretty self-explanatory and carried a mental image of tongue-speaking, moaning, writhing, and frenzy that might not always be accurate and fair but wasn't nearly as fuzzy and ill-defined as socialist. New England? Well, it was "Theosophy" gaining converts at the turn of the twentieth century, said the chronicler of freak cults. Like socialism, Theosophy was problematic when it came to a pithy definition. Just call it the belief in a reservoir of ancient spiritual knowledge and supernatural powers.

So, what was causing such religious freakishness all over the country? "No doctrine so humble but it can find supporters; no prophet so crazy but he can find converts," as the chronicler Alfred W. Greeley concluded in the Birmingham newspaper. One man's opinion, yes, and that man wasn't a theologian, historian, or Freudian. Yet, the reporter's views on the subject were likely not all that different from conclusions that would have been drawn in the day by specialists in those fields. He picked at the cross-grains and separated strands he perhaps clumsily designated "unstable minds," "inevitable prosperity," "civic awakening," and "fervent appeal," which reached across the religious and political divide and the city-country one as well. It was more than "ephemeral hysteria" taking place, he said, and he connected what was going on in his day with the place where it started a hundred years earlier.

"Kentucky's Great Revival" was where the reporter brought his reader-congregants for historical perspective and truth; a truth that, if not setting them free, could at least help in understanding the crazy times in which those readers lived at the turn of the twentieth century. "It was in Kentucky in the early days of the nineteenth century that the 'jerks' had their origin. Then, as now, a wave of moral unrest was sweeping over the country. The war of independence had shattered old ideals that had died a stubborn death with Federalism. French iconoclasm had made thousands of converts in the new nation, and the old Puritan and caste landmarks were submerged. Then as now a multitude of freak social organizations sprang up like mushrooms, their leaders preaching new dispensations and new ideals. And, of course, legitimate religious activities were vitally quickened."

There were traits common to two eras of American history a hundred years apart. That was the estimation of reporter Greeley, and for him those were seen in the aforementioned "jerks" and a "holy laugh" and "barking." "While the progress of this nationwide revival is being conducted in the large cities with conservative enthusiasm, yet reports from isolated country districts show a tendency toward the passionate frenzy that characterized the camp meetings of the first half century of the nation. In the country press now and then one finds reference to the 'jerks' and to the 'holy laugh' in descriptions of successful revivals, and other eccentricities are mentioned as legitimate and commonplace. These uncouth words are the names of practices that have persisted with conservative tenacity in the more backward portions of the country, and the mental states they denote are as highly prized by the 'believers' as Nirvana by the Buddhists."

Journalist Greeley's viewpoint might have been tolerated, even studied, by a big-city industrial audience like Birmingham's, but it's frankly hard to imagine that level of acceptance statewide, especially in his use of "backward" and "mental states" and the audacity of linking heaven-loving Alabama Protestants to Buddhists and Nirvana. No, the collective opinion received through godly tradition cast the camp meeting in a different light than that of Mr. Greeley's "freak cults" compendium in the newspaper, arriving at a different interpretation from secular writing connecting contemporary craziness to the mountaintop experience in Kentucky a century before. By 1884, for example, the camp meeting was already light years away from its dazzling, country-shaping manifestation in Kentucky, but that fact only made the faithful pine that much more for what had been, namely, "camp meetings, *without restaurants and barber shops!*"[9] "There is music, *music*; some with singing, and some alas, without it! But the greatest music which I ever heard, like the combined voices of winds and waterfalls, of thunder and roaring ocean, mingled with the notes of Aeolian harps and the songs of angels, the advent angels and the angels of the covenant, all the orders of angels 'who excel in strength,' and dwell in the immediate presence of God, thrones, principalities and powers, Cherubim and Seraphim! arose from the bosom of a Georgia forest when a great camp-meeting company of earnest men, women and children, like a mighty orchestra, rolled up to the very foot of 'the high throne' the swelling waves of one of our glorious old camp meeting songs."

It was hard to separate fact from fiction. Newspaper serial fiction of the day included the following description in a story line by Eben Rexford regarding frontier revenge on a horse thief: "The forest resounded with the shouts of newly awakened souls, the singing of devout attendants, who hoped by their songs to cheer on those who were wavering between good and evil, and the lusty exhortations of the ministers. One could hear the camp-meeting farther than one could see it."[10] The fiction writer couldn't resist caricatures or types. Take the fictional couple, the Greens. The old woman "was singing that quaint old piece of religious doggerel which most persons who have attended an old-fashioned camp-meeting, or have known an old-time revival, must remember":

O, the sisters want religion!
The brothers want religion!
We've got to have religion—
Glory to the Lamb!

Her lusty singing "rendered her wholly oblivious of all things earthly," comically swaying to and fro, eyes closed, "her old poke-bonnet tipped over on her shoulders, and hanging by its strings, making the worldly-minded and irreverent think of a small mortar aimed skyward, ready to fire off the good old lady's head at the moon." Hubby Bill was "kneeling at the anxious-seat," his "cowardly-heart" frightened by things the preacher said. Bill and the other "seekers" were "groaning and writhing as if the devil hated to let go his hold upon them." Then, this observation by the storyteller, Ebon Rexford: "So the struggle between good and evil went on to the accompaniment of strange sights and sounds which made the scene seem fantastic and unreal enough, to the looker-on who took no active part in it, to be a fragment from a dream."

That, precisely, was the dilemma regarding the camp meeting. It meant one thing for the Zion-destined believer: it was a vision of the fountainhead of Old-Time Religion, worth reliving and resurrecting, or trying to do so, at campgrounds in Alabama with names such as Choctaw, Burgamot, Camp Springs, Healing Springs, Oaktuppa, Rutledge, Hill Chapel, and Wilkey's Springs. Yet, for the worldly, the curious, the grifters—make no mistake about it, those types were always at camp—the scene could be what Greeley said: at best, odd; at worst, dream fragments nightmarish and dismaying. For one thing, "Kentucky's Great Revival" occurred in "A Stronghold of Satan." "No section of the country held out less promise of becoming a religious vineyard than Kentucky. The inhabitants were the cowboys of 1800. Pious visitors were horrified at the drunkenness, vice, gambling, fighting and endless duels. The boatman . . . was more dreaded than the Indians. He was reckless, fearless and law despising, and was commonly described as half horse, half alligator, and tipped with a snapping turtle. Preachers called Kentucky the stronghold of Satan."

The Greeley narrative above requires us to fill in gaps. For example, the reporter mentioned "Red River" but doesn't mention by name the "Second Great Awakening" or "Cane Ridge," the two better-known designations for the groundswell of religion and revival that occurred in the era. Red River was Logan County, Kentucky, where, in 1799, a young Presbyterian preacher, James McGready, held a series of meetings at three small churches he shepherded. Remarkable things came out of the services; their audiences were "strangely moved" is the way Alfred W. Greeley put it. People cried, shouted, begged for mercy, swooned—they were "slain in the spirit" it came to be known. "This was the beginning of a revival that has no equal in the history of the country. The excitement spread like a prairie fire throughout the state. Men fitted their wagons with beds and provisions and traveled fifty miles to camp upon the ground and hear the magnetic minister preach. Other camp meetings were established. Historians of this period say that neither distance, lack of house, nor scarcity of food, nor daily occupations prevailed to keep people away. Families of every protestant denomination hurried to the camp ground, leaving crops half gathered, every kind of work undone. Cabins were deserted and in some large settlements not a single soul remained."

Then, in 1801, the spiritual paradigm occurred for those forest and field meetings that would draw Alabamans and others together for 150 years in hopes of catching lightning in a bottle . . . again! That was Cane Ridge in Bourbon County, Kentucky, *the* camp meeting, attracting stadium-sized crowds before America had stadiums. The figure often cited is twenty thousand Baptists, Methodists, and Presbyterians, who gathered to hear Barton Stone, a Presbyterian, preach—some say it was thirty thousand. Whatever, Cane Ridge was arguably the crest of a Protestant revival remembered as America's Second Great Awakening.[11]

Cane Ridge was in many respects a red, white, and blue religious phenomenon. It's said none other than Daniel Boone gave Cane Ridge its geographical name.[12] What came out of Cane Ridge spiritually was American too, which isn't to say religious excess originated on the ridge, but the jerks, barking, dancing, falling, laughing in such universal and contagious fashion would eventually become hallmarks of American frontier religion in the aftermath of staid Pilgrims and stern Puritan divines. Greeley, the reporter, called the whole "freak cults" phenomenon a "bacillus of innovation," as if the excesses were comparable to a disease. Spiritual disease perhaps! Barton Stone, who saw the jerks firsthand, said this:

> When the head alone was affected it would be pushed backward and forward, or-from- [*sic*] side to side, so quickly that the features

> of the face could not be distinguished. When the whole system was affected I have seen the person stand in one place and jerk backward and forward in quick succession, the head nearly touching the floor behind and before. All classes, saints and sinners, were thus affected. They could not account for it: but some have told me that those were among the happiest seasons of their lives. I have seen some wicked persons thus affected, and all the time cursing the jerks, while they were thus thrown to the earth with violence. Though so awful to behold, I do not remember that any one of the thousands I have seen ever sustained any injury in body.[13]

Stone considered "barking" a form of the "jerks," while dancing and holy laughter was manifested in believers only.

Cane Ridge was remembered in different ways. By 1887, when the peculiar wave of revivalism that started at Cane Ridge had smashed itself against the bulkhead of changing times and society and become diffused within the next era of religious activism, the religious excess that came out of Bourbon County was described as a response to the conditions on the American frontier; how "the people of God were sorely discouraged and bowed down in despair."[14] The revival was the "shaking among the dry bones of the valley." Yet, by the time of Greeley's article in 1907, he was looking at Cane Ridge from the other side. "Travelers in Kentucky at this time say the entire community seemed demented. The high nervous tension and the morbid excitement drove many insane. Men dreamed and saw visions. A peculiar prevalent form of mental disorder was 'treeing the devil.' Men and women who had been aroused to the highest frenzy of excitement fancied themselves dogs, went down on all fours and barked until the voice refused to act. During this outbreak it was a common sight to see a half dozen or more men around a tree barking and yelping. They had 'treed' the devil and were driving his satanic majesty out of the community," is the way Greeley described it to his Birmingham readers.

Cane Ridge was the log meetinghouse. Cane Ridge was the men who were instruments of the Almighty. Cane Ridge was the revival characterized by strange manifestations. All those were subjects of historical treatments during the nineteenth and early twentieth centuries.

Over against those sympathetic and devotional treatments was the perspective of Greeley's "freak cults." It's hard to believe his lumping together of the Cane Ridge camp meeting with cults like the ones he said "germinated and throve" in the area of Vermont and central New York to Pennsylvania—namely, "Dorrillism, Mormonism, anti-Masonry, the Rochester Brotherhood, Spiritualism, the Oneida Community, the Pilgrims, and a host of forgotten minor cults"—would have evoked many intellectual "amens" outside of Birmingham. Plus, he cited that same area as having produced reform movements regarding spirits, as in alcohol, slavery, and women's suffrage. Yes, it was interesting that an area of Christian cults created an environment out of which reform movements could spring. That might be of interest to some, but reform smacked of the world, and the world was the very thing the camp meeting was supposed to keep out. The camp meeting was all about compartmentalization; perhaps it represented the ultimate partition between the world and all things spiritual. The Dorrill guy cited by Greeley? He showed up in Vermont as a refugee (deserter) from the British army and, by 1797, had a group of followers who "were governed in all their conduct . . . 'by the light of nature.'"[15] Dangerous words those, words Greeley understood to mean "a strange influence over women, and [Dorrill's] tastes, like those of most 'prophets,' were strikingly polygamous." "Their Worship an Orgy," declared Greeley in a subheading concerning the Dorrill's group fiddling, singing, and hugging passing for religious worship, "innovations that particularly scandalized the susceptibilities of the pious Vermonters." Sex, demon rum, politics, and social concerns: those had no place at camp! Camp was about spirited preaching, getting right with God, Christian fellowship, and religious excitement, if not frenzy. That Alfred W. Greeley's article was "Special to The *Birmingham News*" was probably a good thing. Had he been a writer-in-residence, one can see where the man might have been criticized if not flailed for failing to separate the Cane Ridge tradition from so many crazy religions.

More than half a century after the Cane Ridge camp meeting and the Second Great Awakening it heralded, Alabamans were still trying to make sense out of not so much the jerks or the holy laugh as the inscrutable nature of time itself; how it never stood still, and the problems that posed. In 1883, when a state paper reported on a camp meeting at McDavid's Station in Florida, the reporting got downright eloquent. "Camp meetings are memorials of that primitive and simple form of worship, which delights the heart to read about, the new fangled ideas of religion is shocked by coming in contact with this mode of worship, the truth is we live too fast to appreciate these time worn methods of obtaining grace. We do not stop to think of the way our blessed fathers sought the way of life, there were no rail-roads to rush them to the camp ground, no facilities to supply their tables daily from the city markets, but they had to hitch the family horse to the carryall, 'Buck and Ball'[16] to the covered wagon, and carry family and stores together, and when they arrived in the neighborhood of the Camp ground they stretched their tents, belled their oxen and abandoned care for worship of the most high."[17]

Now, in modern times c. 1883, just jump on a train with your baggage and don't worry about taking provisions, since the camp train can supply those. If the supply train breaks down or breaks through a trestle, well, just close down the camp meeting! Not so in "old times religion." Back then, such contingencies didn't affect the camp meeting. Indeed, the camp meeting at Williams Camp Ground in Florida was a throwback to those old days, or in that mawkish writer's opinion, a kind of miracle. It would be "remembered on account of its sweet associations, friends long since separated by circumstances met together under the prophetic 'vine and fig tree' to worship once again the master of love. . . . Oh! the hallowed memories that cling to us as we grasp the hand of a friend in the long ago, as we look again into the eyes that laughed and rejoiced when we were in the merry sunshine of youth and happiness, we are reminded that inasmuch as we recognize the companions of early life, that the stern reality of time, has shorn them of their priceless beauty and grace of youth. Sad thought to feel that no morning dew of life will kiss the withered frame of our aged loved ones save when they hold each other to the bosom and dream again of being young. Such is life, aye, be it so, as long as past memories linger with us, we shall hold a reverential regard for Camp meetings." For the anonymous writer, lightning could strike twice; youth could almost be relived, as could Cane Ridge at camp-meeting sites in the wilderness. Yet, not everybody subscribed to that viewpoint. Take a letter to the editor signed "VIATOR," who visited the Little Texas camp meeting in Macon County, "situated about ten miles east of Tuskegee and fourteen miles south of Auburn."[18] VIATOR's letter was years before Greeley's article in the Birmingham newspaper, but he was Greeley-like in his treatment of the camp meeting at Little Texas, only less objective and more ill humored.

> The road from Auburn to Little Texas is a lonely one, plunging deeper and deeper into the solitudes of a great forest, broken only at long intervals by clearings. I was wondering why so inaccessible a spot had been chosen for a place of religious meetings when there occurred to my recollection a fragment of an old hymn, heard in boyhood, but all forgotten save the one line:
>
> "We'll camp awhile in the wilderness."
>
> "In the wilderness" was the refrain of this song of the olden time. It was in intimation of John the Baptist and of the anchorites[19] of a later day that the provinces of this country retired from society into solitary places to worship God. The scarcity of church buildings in the early settlements of the country also had something to do with the organization of camp meetings. It is said to have been a Presbyterian institution, but I think it now peculiar to the Methodist denomination.
>
> In selecting Little Texas for a camp ground its founders displayed excellent judgment, for its site is about as much of a wilderness now as it was forty years ago. The forests surrounding it are primeval, save where the ranks of tall pine trees have been thinned to feed hungry saw mills, thus making room for a ranker growth of scrubby oaks.

For VIATOR, the letter writer, a kind of "survival of the fittest" had taken place in those dense woods. Once upon a time, it seemed, there was what was described as a "notorious 'cross-roads grocery'" where "rustic rowdies" gathered. There, drinking, fighting and murders took place. Now, thanks to the "civilizing influence of the camp-meeting," only a crumbled chimney was left of what the letter writer termed the "grog-shop"—that and stories of the wickedness that occurred at the place. The camp-meeting sanctuary was standing, the place of wickedness long since crumbled.

The victor in that battle of good versus evil in the Macon County woods—the camp meeting—was described this way:

> The site of the camp-ground is a plateau of four or five acres. In the centre stands the tabernacle, which is a large house without walls containing a pulpit and benches for the congregation and fenced to keep out cattle. On the four sides of the grounds, and forming a square, are 'tents,' which are not of canvas, but are rude structures of wood, weatherboarded [*sic*] with rough-edge or sheathing, and white-washed. The tout ensemble is that of the public square of a county seat, with the tabernacle instead of a court-house.
>
> Of the wooded slopes surrounding the square we found innumerable horses, mules and vehicles, giving token of the presence of a large crowd of people.

But it wasn't all rosy, or holy, for the letter writer: "Divine service" was underway when he and his party arrived, so they joined the "great throng" under the tabernacle roof, men on one side, women on the other. "A law like that of the Medes and Persians, forbids the intermingling of the sexes." A man leaning on the fence near his wife was ordered to get back on his side of the tabernacle. The minister, "a man of weak voice," couldn't be heard by the thousand people; not in the open, wall-less, tabernacle; not with the mules braying in the surrounding thickets; not with the babies squalling in the congregation. "The babies always prevailed when they worked together. Let them be harmonious, and they are discordant. I sat by a man who held an infant in his arms. Poor fellow! he could but exclaim at the length of the service. I was sorry for him. I sympathized with him. I knew the grey mare was the better horse at his house. Shake, friend! I observed a woman across the aisle trying to pacify her two-year old son. Being near the pulpit and having strong lungs, he had a great advantage of the preacher. The woman was ingenious and untiring, and at first I was surprised she was not more successful in her commendable efforts to give the preacher a chance, but presently the little boy snatched off his cap with sudden fury, and the secret was disclosed. He had a sorrel top." Noisy, coarse-haired mules and angry, red-headed children: No wonder so many Methodist preachers strained their voices unnecessarily, the letter writer conjectured. It was camp meeting!

Further, when VIATOR left Auburn for the camp meeting in the company of what he called "hospitable citizens," he said "the H.C.'s of Auburn that I met are . . . so exercised . . . by what they characterize as a conspiracy to ruin their college." Whether such worldly concerns could be assuaged by a weak-voiced preacher battling man and beast is anybody's guess, but the letter writer's conclusion was clear. "Have not camp-meetings outlived their usefulness? is a debatable question. An argument in their favor is that they bring together people who do not often attend divine service. An argument against them is that the campground is a place of recreation rather than worship. Young people would undoubtedly object to the abolition of camp-meetings, for under the oaks and in the tents many an unwritten romance begins."

Again, it was about a gradual shift in tone in the camp meeting, about the camp meeting becoming something other than the Cane Ridge event, about it being about something other than religious. "As these meetings are now managed, says a contemporary, they afford the means of summer vacations, at the same time that they provide religious stimulation for the people who throng them. The sermons and exhortations, the fervent prayers and raptuous [*sic*] songs, vary the proceedings of days in which much recreation is found. The camp meeting has become a sort of lengthened picnic, in which many people, young and old, delight to take part, for other reasons than the benefit of their souls. A great deal of worldly ambition enters into it; and the desire for social enjoyment is very manifest."[20]

Once upon a time, in "the groves," Methodists and Baptists planted "fruitful seeds." Now, "the perfected modern camp meeting is a very different thing. It is a summering place, with neat cottages, a police, all the conveniences of life, games and other amusements, and people go thither to occupy abodes of their own; while sometimes shrewd capitalists or real estate speculators make them the means of turning a pretty penny. Instead of the religious feature being the chief one, it nowadays has really become subordinate, in some places, to the social;

and the secular pleasures of the stay at one of these resorts tempt people to it quite as much, certainly, as their desire to take part in devotional exercises." Little wonder that Reconstruction-era Alabama could find a morality tale in the North by which to warn southerners about where things were headed. If you wanted to see how time was corrupting the camp meeting, look no further than Martha's Vineyard in Massachusetts, Sea Cliff in New York, and Ocean Grove in New Jersey. Such retreats were now fancy resorts, made so as a result of subordinating the religious and devotional needs of people to their social needs and secular pleasures. "Modern conveniences"! Those and watered-down religion were to blame. That's what led to "general religious and social sympathy," as opposed to, one might assume, the solitary individual "jerked" into submission to God in whiplash fashion or barking his fool head off at the Devil, sure signs that God was with His people in the American wilderness. It wasn't surprising that the camp meeting was no longer the source it once was for what the newspaper called "religious propagandism."

By the early twentieth century, the camp-meeting experience that once left thousands "slain in the spirit," convulsed by and fitful in the presence of the Holy Ghost, was a source of derision for the likes of "J. Culpepper," who wrote to one of Alabama's largest newspapers and reminisced in humorous fashion about his experiences at camp.[21] "The first one I went to I joined in the 'holy laugh,' which was an old-time expression of superabundance of religion. I was quite young and . . . had unconsciously drifted to the open space about the altar. This was comfortably covered with pine straw. I was soon engaged in some amateur performances of standing on my head, tieing [*sic*] my legs around my neck, etc., which I afterwards learned was against the 'peace and dignity' etc. and for which I paid the penalty on my return. After awhile I noticed long benches of fellows, old, middle-aged and ugly, laughing 'fit to kill themselves.' I thought they were laughing at me and joined in. I didn't know it was 'holy' till I got home." Culpepper passed on other holy rib ticklers to readers:

- The one about the "abnormally ugly" guy who got religion and fell to crying and was approached by a deacon concerning his "facial contortions." To the new convert the deacon said, "I fought through the war. I have traveled through all the States. I have seed many men, but I do say it that crying becomes you the least of any man that I have seed."

- The one about sitting beside a middle-aged bachelor of good repute in the community, when the two of them noticed a weeping young man kneel at the altar. The youth "was too big for his breeches," meaning too ignorant to know that he was too tall and broad for the pants he was wearing. Those pants had straps that went under the shoes—"gallowses"—and upon kneeling, the youth's attire was put under all kind of pressure. That's when the "low, sweet voice of the bachelor" urged Culpepper to kneel on one side of the youth while he kneeled on the other, both with pocketknives out to cut the poor kid's straps. They did and "the poor penitent knew that something had happened but his wild look of distress indicated his fear that the worst had come. . . . The breeches legs, set at liberty by the divided straps, went above the knees like lightning, and in the same moment the poor man was on his feet, with a hunted look." Culpepper said the look of reproach the young man gave both of them was one of being "wounded in the house of his friends," leaving little doubt the poor fellow wouldn't forget the two pranksters in this world or the next.
- The one about him and his friends going to camp meeting "to eat oysters"; how they got into the good graces of the camp-meeting preachers and told the divines that what they were looking for was "special privilege" on the camp grounds, namely, that if Culpepper's company "became exhilarated on too much oyster we didn't want any trouble with police or bailiffs or wardens." The preachers, right then having lunch and drinking something red out of a bottle, seemed to understand. What they were drinking was "iced tea"—that they'd never think of touching wine in public. Culpepper and his friends got acquainted with the iced tea as well, and in no time "hallelujahs" were being raised. "The preachers kept faith with me and, though some of our boys tanked up on the exhilarating oyster 'till it was shameful, not a one of 'em saw inside the lock-up."

It's hard not to believe that "J. Culpepper" was at the very least embellishing his experiences at camp meetings if not completely fabricating them. Either way it showed how far the camp-meeting idea had drifted in the hundred years since Cane Ridge. There were no monkeyshines and pranks in the days of Barton Stone in Bourbon County, Kentucky, when the souls of frontiersmen and the soul of young America were thought to be hanging in the balance. Sinners in the hands of an angry God have no need of humor. "Holy laughter" was about something else all together. "A beautiful penitent kneeling in the altar" and J. Culpepper being outmaneuvered by a widowed old judge for a place next to her? Why, that was making fun of the intrusion of worldly wickedness into holy places! A few years after J. Culpepper made light of what was once a sacred and cherished tradition, the religious expressions that came out of Cane Ridge and other wilderness campsites were remembered as "pioneer hysteria."[22] The pine-straw altars and sawdust trails that changed the face of the country and turned countless thousands toward heaven were already museum pieces, much like the gospel tent the Episcopalians set up in 1876 near Sixth Avenue and Thirty-Fourth Street in Manhattan. It was recalled as being a counterbalance to the Philadelphia Exposition, the first World's Fair held in America, taking place in the centennial year of the signing of the Declaration of Independence. It was said that "the worldly-minded were wandering among the iron-ribbed and jig-sawed buildings" of the Expo, while audiences in the thousands heard "ministers of various creeds" preach in Manhattan and Brooklyn, where another tent was set up. Yet, the Sunday magazine looking back at the camp meeting, noted that services held under tents didn't intrinsically constitute a camp meeting. At best, the Episcopalians were affording visitors a taste of the "old tradition," like a Wild West show acting out snippets of action-packed histrionics. In time, the evangelism of Methodist Peter Cartwright and Presbyterians Barton Stone and James McGready, the preaching that produced barking, jerking, and fits along with salvation, had passed to the likes of Charles Finney and Dwight L. Moody. Their evangelism was described as "winning converts by compassion instead of denunciation." The hysteria waned with the change. By the 1920s and 1930s the Chautauqua, a social institution that gave rural areas access to education and entertainment, appeared as a descendant of the old camp meeting. Preachers, teachers, and musicians were among those who took center stage at the Chautauqua. The country was changing; the camp meeting had to do the same. That was the perspective in 1932, although the change had been set in motion the moment the first soul swooned in Kentucky. "Men and women who lay awake at night listening to the howling of wolves, and who sometimes woke to the horror of the Indians war whoop, could not have the same emotional values as do those whose slumbers are broken chiefly by the honking of motor cars. The modern Kentuckian, turning off his radio in order to get the car out and motor into the nearest city, could not enter a 'gospel tent' in a mood comparable with that of his ancestor, riding many miles from his lonely cabin through the dank and dangerous woods to Cane Ridge, and perhaps uncertain whether his 'shakes' were due to religion or malaria."

Figure 3. The Chautauqua movement started in the nineteenth century with religious roots. By the twentieth century Christian preaching and teaching was part of the education and social movement that included inspirational speakers, lectures, entertainment, and other cultural elements that brought people together. The Chautauqua building is on the left in this postcard of Florala, Alabama, in 1909. Alabama Department of Archives and History.

Still, people don't want to give up on traditions; don't want to admit that nothing—including fervent prayer—can stop the titan time. That's why traditions hang on until they become empty vessels of what they once were, if not objects of scorn, mere relics of the past turned over in the dirt by the trowel of history, and a crumbling chimney marking a spot where righteousness or wickedness once held sway. Perhaps more so, perhaps not, do the people of Alabama resist the irresistible flow from what *was* to the indefinite what's *becoming*. Alabamans were certainly not alone in the desire to hang on to what seemed to be working, to want to pay homage to their fathers and grandfathers by passing along time-worn pathways to salvation, considered the greatest treasure of all. The "Old-Time Religion" was largely thought to be a product of drawing aside and forsaking the world by fleeing to the woods and wilderness glens at appointed seasons. But there existed a dichotomy of sorts in Alabama. The state's lumber and prison camps were places where souls were lost, not saved; hells on earth where some children of God underwent the rigors of damnation at the hands of men who acted as if they were gods in those isolated places. That was part of the clay feet of the camp-meeting experience in Alabama. Yes, campers could flee the world by drawing aside, at least that's what they thought. But the holy camping experience was so insular and self-absorbed that its devotees forgot that the world was the field they were to harvest. Perhaps worst of all, camp meetings could reflect the world the campers claimed to loathe and eschew; the world they "camped" against at appointed seasons. Even Cane Ridge, a heavenly Jerusalem on earth for a few days in 1801, proved to be all too fettered to worldly ways. Barton W. Stone's preaching didn't pass muster as far as the prevailing Calvinism of the day was concerned. Stone and the camp meetings were about *deciding* to turn to God, kneeling in the pine straw and making a decision to follow Christ then waiting on the validation through barks or jerks or laughter. The prevailing Calvinism of the day, however, was about election and predestination. In no time, Barton Stone ran headlong into that Calvinistic wall. He was called to account for his breach of doctrine, left the Presbyterian synod that threatened to sanction him, and eventually left Presbyterianism altogether as a result of the "partyism."[23] In worldly fashion, an argument would emerge over who deserved credit for founding the Christian Church denomination, whose roots were traced to the Cane Ridge revival. Was it Stone or Alexander Campbell?[24]

Still, the retreat idea survived long after the camp meeting had become a shadow of itself. It became associated with "rest and relaxation" and "amusements," as it did when a doctor and his wife turned their "lovely home" into a "modern camp named 'Nikelojo.'"[25] The only conversion mentioned in the news story was that involving the "commodious home" transformed into a camp that would operate during the months of July and August. "This camp is beautifully situated on a high hill four miles south of Jackson, Ala., on the old military road, three miles from the Tombigbee and four miles from the Alabama river." Tennis, swimming, horseback riding, music, and games, along with the "bountiful lunch," were among the pleasures enjoyed by the fifty or so attendees at this pampered day camp. Among the "Grove Hillians" in attendance on Camp Nikelojo's opening day was "Judge Garrett and children." That was "Judge Coma Garrett, Jr." the newspaper gods placed on the same page with Camp Nikelojo's opening, column to the immediate left. It was said Judge Garrett had delivered the chief address at a Woodmen of the World monument unveiled in Linden in nearby Marengo County. The monument commemorated one "J. M. Barkley," a white man, "shot and killed by a negro boy some months ago while a party of white men were purnishing [*sic*] a brother of the negro for stealing from a garage there."[26] There was no escaping the world and its wickedness; it was true for both frontiersmen fleeing into the American wilderness to seek God and molly-coddled day campers seeking nothing more than pleasure, amusement, and distraction. The grisly, detailed story of the killing of J. M. Barkley was on a front page next to the announcement of a two-day 4-H Club Boys Camp, to be held "at Miller's Barn on the river below Nanafalia."[27] A kind of "ten commandments" for campers was listed by the county agent, including:

> 3. Leave all valuables at home such as money, jewelry and fire arms of all descriptions.
>
> 4. You will be expected to obey those in charge of the camp, failing to do so you will be asked to leave the grounds.

5. Only Club Boys and their parents are invited, as "outsiders" will be in the way and often kill the spirit of the camp.

There was nothing new in any of those concerns, all of them going back to the years following Cane Ridge: a suitable campsite (Miller's Barn had "Plenty of deep well water . . . house to sleep in . . . plenty of fish to catch."); what went on in camp regarding behavior; and the presence of outsiders who subverted the camp's intentions. Still, the retreat, the withdrawal, the separation, the camping experience, was the seedbed for galvanizing the solitary soul and groups for the work ahead, be it regarding matters eternal or temporal. In the Depression era, the Civilian Conservation Corps (CCC) was an opportunity for a job, that is, if you were up to "vigorous, healthful, outdoor activity."[28] Indeed, CCC was created "to accomplish constructive, worthwhile work on national and state forests, on parks, and on other lands where such work will contribute to the welfare of the country as a whole. . . . Work to be done includes forest improvement and protection, trail making, soil erosion control, flood control, landscaping and development of recreational areas, and many other similar projects. Work is under the supervision of forestry, park, and conservation representatives of the Federal and state governments."Camp life in the CCC was a "balanced program of work and leisure activities." A young male US citizen between the ages of seventeen and twenty-nine could learn a trade in a CCC camp, as well as participate in recreational and sporting events. A person could even advance to positions of leadership and, in so doing, receive a pay increase up to thirty-six or forty-five dollars a month (of the base thirty-dollar monthly cash allowance, the CCC camper was expected to send about twenty-five dollars to the needy relatives back home.) A six-month "enlistment" in CCC, plus military officers being in charge of the camps, made CCC camping reminiscent of the days when "Tenting on the Old Camp Ground" was a popular, mournful, and war-weary song among Union troops in the American Civil War.[29]

We're tenting tonight on the old camp ground,
Give us a song to cheer
Our weary hearts, a song of home

Figure 4. Even the Depression-era Civilian Conservation Corps had its own version of camp life, the feel of which is evident in this photograph of the 1934 camp in Hacoda, Geneva County. Among many goals, CCC was concerned about the spiritual destiny of America along with the health and well-being of the young men in CCC. Alabama Department of Archives and History.

And friends we love so dear.
Chorus:
Many are the hearts that are weary tonight,
Wishing for the war to cease;
Many are the hearts looking for the right
To see the dawn of peace.
Tenting tonight, tenting tonight,
Tenting on the old camp ground.

When J. C. Fisher used the same tune but turned it into a hymn remembered as "The Old Camp Ground" or "Tenting Again on the Old Camp Ground," the tone was decidedly different:

We are tenting again on the old camp ground,
And we greet in love once more;
Both the hill and the vale the echoes resound,
As we shout the victory o'er and o'er.
Chorus:
We're tenting again, we're tenting again,
Where oft we have met before;
In the Saviour's name we will sing the refrain
On the old camp ground once more.

Again, while camping was anything but a seamless piece of cloth, the various strands making up the idea behind it could be traced to the deep-seated belief that there was something transformative in the experience; something that put people in touch with fundamentals sorely needed by each succeeding generation of Americans who, regrettably, were drawn farther away from key dates and events such as 1776 and 1801. Even when camping's religious moorings shifted to worldly matters it had once sought to escape, it could still be useful in a sociological sort of way.

> Two miles from Grove Hill, Clarke County, a 4-H club camp and community center is being built on 17 acres of land bought and donated by the white citizens of Grove Hill for the colored people of Clarke county [*sic*].

> On this land will be built an auditorium, eight sleeping huts, a work shop, a mess hall, and two bath houses. The auditorium, which will be the hub of the unit is nearly completed.[30]

Yes, it was a $30,000 investment, but more importantly it had a value far beyond dollars and cents where the "colored people throughout the county" were concerned.

> Staying in the camp will give the people an insight into how much more enjoyable their lives would be if their homes were more livable, and there will be instructors to show them how to improve their homes at small cost.
>
> Talks by doctors and nurses on sanitation, health and child care. . . . will do much towards reducing the infant mortality rate, and communicable diseases in the county.

If the gesture proved anything, it was that blindness accompanied camping in the tributaries that spread out from the American frontier. The prominent whites at Camp Nikelojo needed recreation because, well, they just did. The Black kids, on the other hand? Well, it wouldn't be all work and no play for them at camp: "There will be periods devoted to play-acting, ball games, horse shoe pitching, swimming and other recreational activities, of which so many of the race have been deprived." Paternalism was always misconstrued in Alabama as being Christian at heart. So, with a belief in the spiritual values of the wilderness experience, the 4-H Club sent girls off to Suggsville because "Out-of-doors Clarke is too beautiful not to have suitable camping places for its youth."[31] The local Baptists sent their Royal Ambassadors (boys ages nine to sixteen) to a state park at Uriah;[32] once Baptists built Camp Morvin in an unincorporated area of the county, however, it became the site of day-long retreats for children ("nature study, mission study, and fun"[33]) and youth ("swimming, softball, skits, singing, testimonies, supper and the inspirational time"[34]).

It was a familiar refrain, like the chorus of an old hymn. There was something magical, if not sacred, about camping. Even that old

Figure 5. Boys are pictured praying at Camp Rotary's outdoor chapel on July 29, 1954, in Elmore County. Alabama Department of Archives and History.

nemesis, worldliness, was captivated by the experience. Forestry Camp, with boys studying woods-related subjects, shooting on the rifle range, recreating, and cramming to pass a "tough final exam," was a full six days of camping.[35] The camp was underwritten by five companies—"Gulf States Paper Corp., Scott Paper Co., International Paper Co., Marathon Southern Corp., and Coosa River Newsprint."[36] Woodmen of the World Life Insurance Association (WOW), organized in 1890, had various "camps" scattered over Alabama. WOW attendees could hold their "bi-annual head camp meeting" at the Tutwiler Hotel in Birmingham without contradiction.[37] No harm; no foul; the business-oriented Woodmen had symbolic axes, too. "Camp," "resort," "retreat"—eventually these terms came to be used interchangeably in the melting pot created by those with an eye to Zion and those at ease in the world.

> A glade in the mountains in sight of the Dome of Mount Cheaha, the tallest point in Alabama, has been moulded by the brains of far seeing men into a thing of beauty and a joy forever—Shocco Springs. Commodious, airy hotels, to which a new one was added this year, and airy comfortable cottages, all supplied with lights, sanitation, hot and colt [*sic*] water, cluster around a series of gushing springs coming from hills one thousand feet above sea level.
>
> Rest, sleep well, meet congenial people, and have fun—but don't forget the [*sic*] eat well. Here you get real honest-to-goodness cooking that just makes a fellow eat. The water makes you hungry—the air and exercise adds to it, the spirit of the place also helps out so that when the bell rings, you head on a run for the "plate."
>
> Nature made the place a wild and rugged glen whose very roughness made it attractive, while brains and money converted Shocco into an ideal resort.[38]

It's hard not to see a connection between Shocco Springs of the Roaring Twenties, America's Second Great Awakening, and the camp meeting. All the essential elements were present even though Shocco, as a tourist destination, was cited as a collaborative effort between Mother Nature and "brains and money." Still, nature's "spirit" pervaded Shocco through the air and water. Heck, the water was miraculous, having "rare stomachic and curative properties as could be shown by thousands who have experienced it." And who were those who visited for the water, the home cooking, or the back-to-basics experience? They were "Governors, Judges, Congressmen, bankers, flappers, W.C.T.U.'s [Women's Christian Temperance Union] preachers, railroaders, high school graduates, college presidents and widowers." At Shocco Springs you could cut a shine if you wanted to; after all, Shocco "has a large dancing pavilion," or you could enjoy the peace and quiet. A warning, however, had echoes from the old days and the prayer that was no doubt often raised by campers kneeling in the pine straw: "good order must prevail."

Shocco Springs and the old camp meeting came full circle eventually. The connection was the desire to keep embers fanned and burning from the long past era of revivalism that shook America and treed

Figure 6. This Salvation Army Fresh Air Camp at Pickett Springs near Montgomery in 1907 was for the indigent. The 250 working women and children were given two weeks of rest at what was then a thriving resort area in the state. However, in the same way time changed the old camp meeting, Pickett Springs ceased to be a resort draw by World War I. Alabama Department of Archives and History.

Ol' Scratch. In 1948, Alabama Baptists purchased Shocco Springs and turned it into the state's "largest religious retreat center."[39] There wasn't a problem "camping" in the Retreat Lodge in the air-conditioning, or turning aside from the world on well-manicured grounds, any more than there had been for Woodmen of the World "camping" in the Tutwiler or wielding symbolic, useless axes. It wasn't so much about reality as it was the *idea*.

# 2

## "It Was under the Old Fashioned Brush Arbor, Down in the Pine Straw Where Your Mother Was Converted. How She Shouted"

Everyone has an opinion, so it's not surprising that conflicting ideas and viewpoints arise where religion is concerned. One person said this about Burgamot community in Choctaw County: "Our churches are not doing as well as they should, repairs and good pulpit work are much needed."[1] A year later, however, somebody named "Granger" wrote how some might think Burgamot, a community near the Mississippi line fifteen miles or so southwest of county seat Butler, had been annexed by Mississippi, what with the appearance that not much was going on. That wasn't necessarily so, said Granger. "Though behind in some things, we are not backward in spiritual affairs. Great zeal is manifested in all things pertaining to the church. The two churches, Mt [*sic*] Hebron and Oak Grove, have consolidated; and we intend to build a first class church house."[2] While this isn't an attempt to explain two differing opinions regarding the spiritual condition of souls in Burgamot—the first letter was written in 1882, the second a little over a year later in 1883—note that in between the letters' appearances something occurred. "The enthusiasm at the Burgamot camp ground is said to have reached a boiling heat. The people during one entire day, were so much excited that it was impossible to preach to them. From sunrise to sunset, one continued shout, went up from the mouths of the converts. Whatever our misfortunes in other respects religion is on a boom in the county, as the recent meeting at

Butler, and Burgamot camp ground abundantly prove."[3] The week before, this notice was no doubt a reference to the same religious "boom" in Choctaw County: "Camp meeting commenced last Saturday at the Oaktuppa camp ground. A great many from Butler went down Sunday, but on account of the meeting here, remained but one day. The attendance is said to be good; and the sermons to be having a glorious effect. Religion has been shed abroad in the hearts of the congregation."[4]

The spiritual "box-score" was an important part of reporting on camp meetings:

> Last week our readers were informed that the camp meeting in this vicinity had resulted in the conversion, of what we stated on conjecture, 40 or 50 souls. Since then we have learnt that the number of white persons who professed religion at the camp meeting was 44, and of the colored 48, making 92 in all."[5]

> Thirty-seven were added to the church and seventy-four came forward and testified to having received pardon. It is supposed, that between ninety and one hundred were converted, as many left without publicly acknowledging the fact.[6]

> A camp meeting has been held by the Methodist Church during the last few days at George's settlement, about five miles from Chunchula [Mobile County]. . . . The average number in attendance has been 300.[7]

> The camp-meeting at the Choctaw camp-ground closed last Wednesday evening. The meeting was largely attended and the services very impressive. A large number of persons professed religion and 10 were admitted into the church.[8]

> The camp-meeting at Camp Springs was well attended, we learn that the singing of the children was very fine. Sixteen joined the church and 20 concluded it was time to turn over a new leaf.[9]

> The camp meeting at the Choctaw Camp Ground closed on last

> Tuesday night. Between fifteen and twenty accessions to the church are reported.[10]

> All the tents and bungalows were filled with campers and the average daily attendance was from 800 to 1500.[11]

> Camp-meeting at Choctaw Camp ground was brought to a close on yesterday morning. We understand there were a number of conversions, including some of the toughest cases in the county.[12]

At the end of the nineteenth century, camp meetings were destinations, and preachers were stars in heavenly circuits. Railroads sold round-trip tickets to camp meetings. For example, the Mobile and Birmingham Railroad offered a round-trip fare of $5.15 from Whatley in Clarke County to a campground near Biloxi, Mississippi.[13] In Selma, a round-trip ticket to a camp meeting at Cox's Station, ticket good for Sunday only, could be purchased at the Broad Street depot for $1.10.[14] It was expected that a large crowd would avail itself of the offer since "Camp meetings are greatly to the liking of many Selmians, as past experiences have fully proven." An ad on the same page of the newspaper under the name of railroad agent C. H. Lavender announced excitedly, "Ho! For the Camp Meeting!" That was the same modern contrivance credited with putting an end to "the essential joy . . . of the life of the pioneer," namely, the system of railroads that pushed into the American wilderness and brought development in its wake.[15] Those were the words of Bill Nye, a renowned nineteenth-century humorist and journalist. His sarcasm notwithstanding, one has to wonder how many readers mistook Nye's razor-sharp wit for gospel and endorsed his diatribe against trains and, as it were, canned peaches. The train? "It has driven out the long-handled frying pan and the flapjack of twenty years ago, and introduced the condensed milk and canned fruit of commerce. Along the highways, where once the hopeful hundreds marched with long-handled shovel and pick and pan, cooking by the way thin salt pork and flapjacks and slumgullion, now the road is lined with empty beer bottles and peach cans that have outlived their usefulness. No landscape can be picturesque with an empty peach can in the foreground, any more than a lion would look grand in a red monogram horse blanket and false teeth." Here was this modern thing, this killer of the frontier's "essential joy" and "fun," according to Nye, offering round-trip tickets on rails to the past; the cherished past that some understood still survived in the camp-meeting experience of that day. Just how much change had actually taken place from the days of heavenly Cane Ridge was open to discussion. Were the candidates for probate judge of Choctaw County, who just happened to show up at the camp meeting, there for religious or political reasons? Was it "an eye to business on that occasion," or were they "glad to see their old friends and get acquainted with new ones"?[16] The newspaper seemed to attribute mixed motives at best to the politicians.

The preachers, however, weren't lumped with the railroad's theft of the pioneer soul, an ignominy the automobile would eventually share, or the motives of worldly men who congregated to pump hands for political gain. No, the preachers were still holding the line and protecting the sacredness of the camp meeting; men like the "Rev. Dr. Wadsworth, presiding elder of this Methodist circuit," who'd just finished a camp meeting in Clarke County.[17] "The eloquent and devoted Doctor, than whom there is not an abler divine in the Methodist Church, nor a purer Christian in the land, is laboring unceasingly in his field of duty. Wherever he goes he wins golden opinions from all men." The same was said about Dr. A. S. Andrews, who was greeted by two thousand campers at Little Texas Camp Ground in Macon County, "grand rallying point of the Methodists of East Alabama."[18] "The Doctor fully sustained himself in his well-earned reputation, and was followed by the Rev. W. C. McCoy, of the North Alabama Conference, in an eloquent appeal in behalf of the Southern University at Greensboro. . . . Dr. McCoy delivered on Sunday evening a most powerful sermon. He threw his whole soul and being into his discourse, and under the inspiration of the hour the effect was very telling."

At this point an introduction is in order. There is, hanging on the wall to my right as I watch television, a painting by my wife of my great-great-grandfather, the Rev. Joseph Harvey Fendley, the painting based on a grainy photograph of the man. Dead since 1927, the Reverend Fendley was highly esteemed in his day as a Baptist minister and

Figure 7. The Rev. Joseph Harvey Fendley, Confederate soldier turned gospel preacher and church planter. From the collection of the author.

church planter in southwest Alabama. It was a big deal in my family when I entered the ministry and took up the clergy mantle he wore nearly eighty years before I was born. How the reverend might have felt when I ultimately left the ministry and became a newspaper journalist I can't say. The painting offers no clues in that regard. I often stop and look him in the eye. I can't tell if he's staring—glaring—at me while I watch *Netflix*, critical of both my vocational choice and love of horror movies, or looking toward me, gazing over my head into oblivion. It matters not which, but on a number of occasions, some of them as a green ministerial student, sometimes in recognition of the historical connection and sometimes not, I filled the pulpits of some of those small, piney-woods churches the reverend established and served long before I came along. I followed in the footsteps of a holy spirit who was my ancestor and who adorns the wall of my living room today the way he no doubt shares my soul-house, a duplex with me in one side, he in the other. He was born in 1836 in Wilcox County, Alabama, and I bring the reverend into discussion here for two reasons.

First, his life offers firsthand general information concerning the days when it was hoped that the embers of Cane Ridge could be fanned into a repeat—a second coming of a Great Holy Ghost Revival that could shake the foundations of (if not the country) at least a county or area where it was deemed sin and corruption was rife and men in need of a good divine shaking or jerking. I say firsthand information since the Rev. J. H. Fendley wrote a few homily-like observations or meditations on subjects such as "Heaven" and "On the Incoming Year of 1906" that have ended up in my possession. One of those writings, however, is especially pertinent here. "Sixty Nine Years In The World" was started in 1905, and the reverend purposed to set out his life story. Hard as it is to believe, the man with the sphinx-like eyes must have possessed a sense of humor because the setup for the life story he intended went this way: He wouldn't be like the preacher who took for his text "The world, flesh and the Devil." The sneaky punch-line: "The preacher stated to his audience that he would pass briefly over the world, touch lightly on the flesh and hasten on to the Devil." The Reverend Fendley, however, purposed that the "text" for his life story would "pass briefly over childhood, touch lightly on boyhood and hasten on to old age." In telling his story, he proposed to touch on such topics as customs of the nineteenth century, politics and religion of the era, and other matters. As far as I know, he never got past boyhood in his account since I have nine single-spaced pages that somebody typed. If there's more I don't know about it; likewise, I assume what he wrote was never published or got a reading outside my family. The value of what was handed down is that it recounts the tone of pioneer days in Alabama and, thus, the days of camp meetings and brush arbors.

He had an eventful boyhood, to be sure. The reverend was born in a log cabin near Sunny South. He went to school in a schoolhouse where the cracks between the logs served as windows. He found and killed twenty-three rattlesnakes at one time with another boy. He burned down the family house and all its contents in 1842 while galloping through the house straddling a chair and waving around a lightwood torch. His family moved to Mississippi in 1843 by covered wagon pulled by two oxen, Buck and Darbe. Feeling his oats, he insisted on mastering Buck and Darbe by riding on the wagon tongue and geeing and hawing the animals and got run over by the wagon after it hit a stump and he fell beneath it. He got into a scuffle at age nine—the reverend called it a "fist and skull fight"—with another boy over politics and daddies, as the reverend's father was a Henry Clay and Whig man, and the other boy's daddy a Democrat and James K. Polk man. He saw his first Mormons and refuted Mormonism the rest of his days. He saw his first stagecoach, it carrying mail and passengers, its arrival announced along the way by a "trumpet or bugle." He caught his first fish in the Tombigbee River from the Mississippi side ("a 'Red Horse,' a scaley [*sic*] fish"). By means of wagon and ol' Buck and Darbe, he came back to Alabama in 1845. He saw five neighbor boys headed off to the Mexican War, one of whom, while on guard duty, would shoot and kill a Mexican boy and face a court-martial at the war's end but was released. He experienced preaching in different homes, and the singing, praying, shouting, and crying made him think everybody was ready right then for heavenly transport.

Remember the J. Culpepper story recounted herein from 1904, in which godly J. Culpepper and another good Christian took advantage of a weeping young man kneeling at the altar—a young man too big for his breeches? Well, the reverend had a similar experience. One time, at one of those long ("protracted") revival meetings that could go on for weeks, the services split between a brush arbor and meetings held in various homes, the boy tagged along one night with his father. His father wore a "blue pigeon tailed coat and lapel breeches and a pair of homemade shoes," the reverend "a calico gown, with two buttons, one at my neck and the other on the belt about the middle of my waist." The gown was full at the breast and hung down to the calves of his legs, "tight as Dicks [*sic*] hatband," as he recalled in 1905. And he wore his father's hat. It wasn't a day when mirrors were exactly handy, so the reverend couldn't see the figure he cut the way others could. At the meeting everybody got a good laugh at his expense, especially since his mother, "a stickler for cleanliness," had scrubbed his knees with warm water and lye soap, and they were more than a little red as a result.

It was one small glimpse into both the logistical and spiritual uneasiness involved in southern religion of the day. The day in question included this sequence. Ride a horse bareback behind his father to the meeting; hold the prized hat in his hand all the way for fear of it coming off and getting lost; at the meeting not knowing what to do with his father's hat upon reaching a decision to kneel at the mourner's bench, a decision he wrestled with before going forward. Why not go forward? "I felt that I was very well dressed, and felt like I ought to go up." Holding his father's hat in one hand, he offered the other hand to the preacher, knelt, got up, and almost put the hat on too soon, and, once the meeting was adjourned, jumped up on a stump to take his place on the horse behind his father and the hat went flying off and had to be retrieved. Then, ride home in the dark feeling sick and ashamed and facing a sleepless night. Why? "I didn't know whether I had religion or not." The hat protocols notwithstanding, the reverend recalled it this way: "I was in a bad fix." Sometimes you do what you think is right only to discover that now you had to join the church or be looked upon as a hypocrite. As he recalled, he didn't go to the revival meeting the following night, and it was years before he went forward again asking for prayer. Also, "I have never liked to wear peoples [*sic*] things since."

There were other life incidents that would become lessons, some harder than others to take in. He lost a brother in 1849, another in 1852, a third in 1856. When he was about twelve, he suffered with a bout of pleurisy; it was diagnosed by an old man who was a preacher *and* a medical man. The preacher/doctor bled him with a "thumb lancet" and "blistered" his side. His father got his first slave, Isaac, from his grandfather. The reverend had his best day picking cotton: 436 pounds in a day near Yellow Bluff landing. He once dug an eighty-foot well. Picking cotton and well-digging probably wasn't as difficult as overcoming his admitted bashfulness with the opposite sex. One night, while riding home on horseback after telling some girls goodnight—no doubt the fair sex on his boyish mind—he struck a limb and lost his hat. Always the hat trouble! There were the inevitable bad habits that boys pick up: chewing tobacco; the occasional sips of "Johnnie High"; the "twistifications" at dance parties; the card-playing. And there was the heartbreaking reality of being the ungrateful son and having to sit through the tearful admonishments and pleas of godly parents concerning those youthful indiscretions and sins.

The reverend, by 1905 and probably long before, was adept at taking little vignettes from Alabama frontier life and turning them into wisdom for the ages. He killed a squirrel, ran to the house with his prize, but forgot his gun—"an old flint and steel single barrel shotgun"—left in "the crack of the fence." Lesson: "we are liable to loose [*sic*] the presence of mind in our success, and also loose sight of some things of value and importance." The family horse got loose one night and was "progging around the yard" when it stumbled over the family dog. The dog let loose a "frightful yell," scared the horse right back, and both animals ran off in the same direction. "[A]n unexpected approach leads to excitement," the reverend intoned, like King Solomon.

The most difficult lesson, and likely the most impactful one of the man's life, wasn't recorded in that 1905 recounting of his life, which, as noted, abruptly ended with a period before he got close to covering his full sixty-nine years of life to that point. But a letter to his family survived, dated September 24, 1863, and written from Ringgold, Georgia, in the northwestern corner of that state. The reverend, then twenty-seven years old, was in a field hospital, having been wounded at the Battle of Chickamauga, a bloody encounter between Union and Confederate troops that involved the states of Georgia and Tennessee. The letter, discovered by family in 1923, a few years before the reverend died, was addressed to his father, Tully Fendley, his mother, Webb Eliza, and "Sisters and Brothers." The letter's contents are what one would imagine: "O Pop, you have no idea what feelings I have had and have now, and what disasters and suffering is here!" He tells his father about the fates of soldiers he names, as if Tully Fendley knew them personally and could have known them if they were Alabama boys. So and so and so and so wounded or missing; this officer and that killed on the field; so and so had his leg cut off; he "reckons" so and so is dead but wounded for certain. "They cut us all to pieces." He closes with "O, my heart is full. O God help us I pray." His father died the following year and never saw his son, who was in other famous battles of the American Civil War, come home in 1865. The reverend was paroled and took up farming. Tully Fendley never saw his son leave the dirt clods and plowing behind in 1869 and become an ordained minister.

That's the second reason the reverend is included here in the camp-meeting discussion. Search as I may, I could find no reference to the Reverend Joseph Harvey Fendley preaching at any camp meeting. That doesn't mean he didn't, but one thing seems abundantly clear: the hopes of a spiritual bounty from the Holy Ghost was the inspiration behind and goal for the planning and preparation of the camp meeting, the reason to be an on-site camper, and worth all the trouble involved to get to pray in the pine straw. But the ghosts of Confederate dead were an unspoken part of the southern camping experience as well, cultural specters perhaps not consciously invoked, but present nevertheless. I believe that can be proven conclusively, but at this point note the following concerning the reverend:

> The Board of Pension Examiners will meet at the Court House of Clarke County, on the first Monday in July, 1915, and remain in session ten days, for the purpose of examining any new applicant desiring Confederate Pensions, and those who have been stricken from the roll by the State Board of Pension Examiners may appear before us at that time with their witnesses and show cause, if any they have, why they should be re instated [*sic*] on the pension roll and placed in the class from which they were stricken, as provided by an Act of the Legislature, approved February 19, 1915.
>
> J. W. Armistead, M.D.,
> J. H. Fendley, C.V.
> Co. Board of Examiners.[19]

I'm of the opinion that the reverend wasn't a dichotomist or quarry thinker; he saw the world as one and under the One God. As such, for him, any endeavor or pursuit was a Christian one, and it seemed the reverend likely practiced what he preached. Thus, it's up to me, his wayward great-great-grandson, to try to prove a point by making a point he likely wouldn't agree with, namely, that the man wasn't shy about taking on *secular* pursuits. J. H. Fendley, "Confederate Veteran," advocated for Confederate pensioners the way he did for "aged and Infirm Ministers, their widows and Orphans" at a church meeting in 1887.[20] Likewise, when an acquaintance running for public office in neighboring Choctaw County came under suspicion regarding morals, the reverend took up his pen to underscore the commandment against bearing false witness, and bolstered his case with the fact "that I have been engaged in the preaching of the gospel for a period of fifty years."[21] Also, he never shied away from ties to his former brothers-in-arms, even the most unlikely of them.

When E. P. Chapman died in Grove Hill on March 28, 1920, at age ninety, he was remembered as a man who spent his life in the Grove Hill area, where he was known far and wide as a business and political leader.[22] A Confederate veteran, he was "one of the first to answer his country's call, serving four years with Wirt Adams' Cavalry in Mississippi and North Alabama." Chapman had been county tax assessor and sheriff during the 1850s and, in 1906, became president of the Bank of Grove Hill. He was president of "Camp Calhoun, U.C.V." in nearby Jackson, the local Confederate veterans' organization. What's noteworthy here is that E. P. Chapman was a member of the Universalist church and credited with giving it a foothold in the area. Certainly, Universalism was an odd duck in the presence of Clarke County revivalism's standard drumbeat of eternal damnation, wielded like a cudgel to bring human beings to their senses and salvation. If a loving God is going to ultimately redeem all humankind, give everybody a free pass, what's the fun or need in counting souls saved at churches like Elam, New Prospect, or Bassetts Creek, or at camp meetings, where salvation was validated through swooning, barking at the Devil, and holy laughter? Yet, the escort of honor that preceded E. P. Chapman's casket consisted of eight brother Confederate veterans, one of whom was the Rev. J. H. Fendley, who met his first Mormon as a kid and railed against what he called Mormons' "deluded belief" in his memoir. Apparently, the standard, "Blest Be the Tie that Binds," written by a Baptist who was converted by a Methodist, held true for those bound by a Lost Cause and the loss of precious southern blood, denominational lines be damned!

Burying, marrying, church centennials, revivals, singings, dinners-on-the-ground, ordinations, and an array of Baptist associational meetings: the reverend's religious life had an *administrative* streak running through it—an orderliness. Sure, he could preach on First Thessalonians 5,[23] a chapter full of admonitions for Christian living. Don't quench the Spirit! Don't despise prophecy! Leave evil alone! But looking back, sources also find him addressing such matters as "Can Christians Consistently Neglect Church Attendance?"[24] "What Constitutes a Missionary Baptist Church?"[25] "Should non-church goers and non-church supporters be retained by the church?"[26] "Woman's Work and Missions."[27] Those weren't exactly topics that would set the sinner's hair on fire or make the Devil flee up a tree. But they underscore the point that "church" life was one thing, camp-meeting life something different. Under a roof with pews or benches, an altar, and set spiritual rules to follow and obey; out under the open sky, in the "wilderness" on your knees in the pine straw, and at the mercy of the Holy Spirit; well, the outcomes could vary as could expressions of the Christian life. The camp meeting's feverish excitement had a magnetic attraction for all types and influences. Not all who were drawn to the fire were straight arrows, like the reverend, or grounded camp-meeting "stars," like the "Rev. Dr. Wadsworth," presiding elder of a Methodist circuit, who doubtlessly had to take care of administrative matters as well, or the Reverend W. C. McCoy of the North Alabama Conference, who could challenge two thousand Methodist campers at Little Texas to support a church-related school, then apparently blister them with the gospel.

The camp-meeting tradition, written, as it were, on fleshy tablets of the human heart, wasn't receptive to changes from planes, trains, and automobiles, especially when those changes involved old tried-and-true ways of bringing God and worshiper together. No, the Christian heart was stubborn—call it *perseverance* in Christian terms—and less likely to surrender to worldly change. The camp meeting was about the human heart's condition; on one hand, its intractable nature in refusing to cooperate with God; on the other, God overcoming its stubbornness and setting tortured souls free to dance and laugh and bark to beat the band. Such heart-felt recollections wouldn't be surrendered without a fight. Consider the following reminiscences that appeared in 1910 in connection with the Bluff Springs Camp Meeting in Coffee County:

> S. Felder says: "We cannot imagine any one thing calculated to do more real, lasting good than this old time camp meeting. It will bring all the people together and revive that old time religious fevor [*sic*] for which this section was long ago famous."
>
> Leave off your fine clothes and stiff airs and come to the brush arbor where you will kneel in the pine straw.
>
> It was under the old fashioned brush arbor, down in the pine straw where your mother was converted. How she shouted.
>
> The old fashioned brush arbor, the old fashioned pine straw; the old fashioned dirt fire stands.
>
> The assembled multitudes, the blazing fires, the neighing horses, the rumbling wagons, the swelling songs, the fervent prayers, the triumphant shout—an old fashioned camp meeting.
>
> Old time religion makes old time folks old time children of God, with old time heaven on earth.[28]

The theme of the devoted, transformed heart was peppered throughout the story of the Dixons Mill camp meeting. That story appeared in 1932, twenty years after the Marengo Union Camp Meeting was established and long before this author looked skyward in his youth and saw secular dove descending. The article defined the camp meeting thusly: "A camp meeting is a religious gathering for prayer, instruction, exhortation, etc., held in an encampment formed in a wood, grove, or field, generally continued for a week or more."[29] A definition as good as any and the story behind this one camp meeting's tradition was equally good in the presentation of its inspiration and bliss.

The nonsectarian camp meeting in Dixons Mill, one "in which Methodists, Baptists and Presbyterians unite[d]," started with a revival service led by two young "student evangelists" out of Kentucky and Georgia. The service was held at a school house in the Miller community. There, Miss Willie M. Thomas was the teacher. When the reporter visited the home of "Miss Willie" and her sister to talk about the camp meeting, he found it "a house of hospitality, culture and Christian living, a home by the highway which is a blessing to the community." The young evangelists—"Evangelist Stewart was from Georgia, and Evangelist Seevers from Kentucky"—"in 1911 sowed evangelical seeds which blossomed and fruited into a harvest of new born souls." Stewart did the preaching, Seevers conducted the singing. "These consecrated young students were no high powered, commercialized evangelists, but had their hearts in their work as is evidenced by the fact although they were holding meetings to get money to continue their ministerial studies, at the close of revival services at Miller school house they tithed the free will offering and returned $10 to Miss Janie Skinner, of Miller, now engaged in Y.W.C.A. work in Oklahoma, to establish an annual union revival work." The action of the student evangelists were like a modern-day parable. Indeed, the newspaper referred to it as an example of the "Widow's Mite," a teaching of Jesus concerning what a small amount means when given by a devoted heart: "The widow's mite has come ringing down through the ages to inspire consecrated giving, and the $10 gift of the two unselfish young ministerial students has been blessed a thousandfold. The gift became the nucleus around which was built the camp ground at Dixons Mills. It was the wish of Miss Thomas and her sister, Mrs. Miller, who had commenced their careers as teachers in the old Dixons Mills Academy that the camp grounds be located in it, not only for sentimental reasons but from the fact two of the principal roads in the section crossed in the village, and that a railroad was nearby. However, the thought behind these advantages was their deep desire for a spiritual awakening in the community."

The campgrounds were all Currier & Ives and Norman Rockwell, according to the reporter. "The day we visited the camp grounds was a glorious one. It is located on beautiful shady ground, comprising several acres, close to the old mill pond, an ideal place for a camp meeting. The running water was easily accessible. A vacant seven-room house was available for transients, the rooms being rented for 25 cents a night. A restaurant was operated to furnish meals at a very low cost. Those coming merely for the day were asked to bring their lunches." Likewise, the announcement that advertised the Dixons Mill camp meeting, typically held from August 1 through August 10, was reproduced in the article: "Realizing that in union there is strength, a number of the various denominations of Marengo, Clark [*sic*] and Wilcox Counties have planned to cooperate in holding a large union or camp meeting to be located centrally. Services will be conducted under a large tent and arrangements have been made for those attending from a distance to camp on the grounds and thus enjoy the meeting uninterruptedly."

Just because camp-meeting roots went back to the American frontier and wilderness, back to a simpler life and times that succeeding generations longed to relive through camping, doesn't mean what happened in more or less spontaneous fashion at Cane Ridge could be recaptured with ease. No, it wasn't all on the Holy Ghost to make a successful camp meeting; it took planning and preparation. The lead-up to the 1910 camp meeting at Bluff Springs, cited previously for sentimentality regarding brush arbors and pine straw and triumphant shouts, was blunt about the other side of the spiritual equation for camp-meeting success. That was human preparation, including something as simple as bringing a tent or building one out of boards, to "Bear your own expenses."[30] Charity had its limits at camp meetings, according to the aforementioned Reverend H. B. Urquhart, pastor of the Methodist Church in Elba.

> Everybody pays their own expenses. Don't expect your friends to take care of you.
>
> The self-sustaining plan is the proper thing. No one will then impose upon another.
>
> Messrs Carnley, Symonds, Rowe and Carmichael were appointed a committee to solicit funds for necessary expenses at the meeting Tuesday morning of the arrangement committee.

Juxtaposed with "Bring your cook stove and provisions, and live in camp for ten days worshipping God. And endeavoring to turn sinners from their way. Come, sinners, camp with us and we will do you good,"[31] was the practical side, "Wood for cooking can be had for the hauling—a small load will last the entire meeting. If you do not wish to haul your wood two families can unite and buy a two-horse wagon load of wood for a dollar; or three families as the case may be." The Holy Ghost could come and go as He pleased, but campers planning to tent on the banks of Pea River needed to drop "a postal card" to the Reverend Urquhart. Also, it couldn't be said enough: "The camp meeting will run on the self-sustaining plan: that is every one [*sic*] will be expected to bear his own expenses."

"Self-sustaining plan": It was the same phrase used in 1879 concerning Union Camp Ground in Clarke County. John A. Green, in a letter to the editor, noted that he'd been asked several times if a camp meeting would be held in September. Yes, he replied, but "every man must do his duty in this great work."[32] "I do not believe in making a few good men and women bear the burden of a camp-meeting. Every one ought to bear his part. Those who live near enough ought to tent; even those who live several miles off ought to tent if they can. Those who are not able to tent by themselves ought to get one or two families to join with them and put up a joint tent. Those who cannot do this ought to help furnish the provision and other necessities for a tent. By doing this, the camp-meeting can be carried on successfully without much expense to any one [*sic*]." Closer to the Union camp-meeting date, the same John A. Green said the event, which would "commence Friday before the 4th Sunday in September," would operate "on the self-sustaining plan."[33] "We mean, by this, for every one [*sic*], except the preachers, to take care of himself. Those who do not tent must go prepared to help furnish one, or take care of themselves." Thus, the camp meeting, which some felt was "a transitory scene of the millennium,"[34] was changing; it had to. At Dixons Mill, what began with two saintly ministerial students tithing what amounted to a Widow's Mite had, by 1929, become an "association" that "formed a stock company" to buy the grounds—eighteen acres—where the Marengo Union Camp Meeting was held.[35] The association bought the camp tabernacle and other buildings, but twenty-two cottages were privately owned. That led to this observation concerning Dixons Mill: "From a camp meeting of tents it has become a camp meeting of wood." The article mentioned officers of the association and its committees, advisory and finance. Besides Dixons Mill, there were people filling offices and committee slots from such places as Thomasville,

Sweet Water, Linden, Pine Hill, Selma, Tuscaloosa, and Thomaston. However, a connection to the primal wilderness and early Methodist circuit-riders held on, even as the camp meeting became as much about earthly business matters as the mysterious movement of the Spirit, as much about Humanity's doings as God's in pulling off successful tenting.

Figure 8. "Gwine to Alabam." This couple photographed around 1900 could have been on their way to a Alabama camp meeting since the photographer captured the necessary ingredients of the religious camper: hale and hearty pioneer types, who hitched up their wagons to their animals, threw what they needed in the wagon, and headed off for isolated spots or wilderness areas to live for days or weeks with fellow believers seeking an experience with the Lord. Alabama Department of Archives and History.

Consider the "Statement of Receipts and Expenses [of the] Marengo County Camp Meeting Association Year 1926" that appeared in print;[36] 1926 turned out to be a particularly tumultuous year in one regard for the Dixons Mill camp meeting. Among the expenses reported by the five-member Finance Committee were such uninspiring items as the following: $114.95 for roofing and nails; $691.30 for the "Light Plant"; $82.25 for ice; $112. 91 for wiring the camp grounds; $77.50 for labor involved in hauling sawdust and benches and the like. Factor in the $2,093.45 paid to the superstar evangelist, and there was a "Total Deficit" of $149.49 against the cash collections and other income sources. That, however, was worldly bookkeeping; it had nothing to do with the heavenly ledger, the bottom line of which was something altogether different. How can you put a dollar amount on an *idea* that lived on in sentimental flourishes and pastoral sketches?

> Way down in the heart of Marengo County, where the watermelons are the sweetest[,] fried chicken the juciest [*sic*], and the trees are the shadiest and greenest in the hot summer months, is an attractive little county town that has been put on the map since 1912 when the first services of the Marengo Union Camp Meeting was selected for this prominence. . . .
>
> [T]he large tabernacle built in a natural park of lovely Southern trees and shrubs. The notes of the native birds are sometimes mingled with the harmony of the orchestra.[37]

As noted, while preachers by and large were portrayed for over a century as instruments upholding the same gospel that brought God to the American frontier and conquered its wilds and wild ways, Barton Stone and others preaching at Cane Ridge were immediately swept up in, among other things, theological disputations regarding Calvinism and arguments over ecclesiastical jurisdictions, thus resulting in church schism in the creation of the Cumberland Presbyterian Church from expelled members of the Presbyterian Church U.S.A. The preachers were as susceptible to the warping and bending of the world as the camp-meeting tradition was in going from tents to wood, from going from nomadic strangers in a strange land (tenters) to citizens at home in earthly Zion (cottages). In that regard, note two luminaries from the introduction who appeared in Marengo County more than once to preach at the camp meeting: Bob Jones and Gypsy Smith.

# TEN DAYS OF RECREATION AND INSPIRATION

## MARENGO COUNTY UNION CAMP MEETING

## Dixons Mills, Ala., August 11-21.

**CAPT. W. C. BLASINGAME**
**of the U. S. Public Health Service.**

**Capt. Blasingame has an important message to deliver on subjects of vital importance. Everyone should hear him.**

**J. B. GREEN**
**General Secretary of the Alabama Sunday School Association**

**Mr. Green will conduct special services for Sunday School workers.**

Figure 9. This newspaper ad announcing the upcoming Marengo County Union Camp Meeting in 1921 reflected the changes that had occurred in the camping idea over the years. "Recreation" and "Inspiration" were given equal footing. There would be spirited preaching, yes, but camp-meeting goers would also hear about matters related to public health and receive training as Sunday School teachers. The announcement appeared in the *Democrat-Reporter* newspaper in Linden, Alabama, on August 4, 1921.

In the late nineteenth and early twentieth centuries, references to "Gypsy Smith" in Alabama newspapers numbered in the hundreds if not thousands, nearly always in relation to camp meetings, revivals, and religious rallies. The trick was to know the difference between three evangelists so-named. The most famous Gypsy Smith was arguably Rodney Gypsy Smith, a British evangelist who crossed the Atlantic dozens of times to hold religious meetings in the United States. That Gypsy Smith had been a Salvation Army evangelist at one point, a "captain" in General William Booth's spiritual army. But that Gypsy Smith had a son, Albany, who also became an evangelist. So, there was Gypsy Smith Sr. and Gypsy Smith Jr. But when the *Birmingham News* carried the big article on the Dixons Mill camp meeting in early 1932, it gave a long list of preachers who'd held sway at the event over the years, including Gypsy Pat Smith in 1926 and Gypsy Smith again in 1927.

The Gypsy Smith referenced was "Captain Gypsy Pat Smith," no relation to the other two, a man of "magnetic personality and an interesting career who was returning in 1927 to conduct the camp meeting from July 22 to August 7."[38] And why not a return engagement? During the 1926 camp meeting, he preached to ten thousand people over one weekend, and the 2,000 automobiles parked around the event were the largest number people had ever seen at Dixons Mill.[39] Gypsy Pat Smith is the one paid the $2,000-plus cited above. The crowd included visitors from Birmingham, Selma, Meridian, Mississippi, York, Demopolis, Montgomery, Camden, and other towns. One night Gypsy Pat Smith spoke on the subject "Experience of three years with God and man on the firing line in France." It was part of the evangelist's personal testimony—his "interesting career."

Gypsy Pat Smith was born "of purest Rominy [*sic*] stock and lived the life of a nomad until he was sixteen years old."[40] "The story of the man's life reads like a romantic novel . . . born in a gypsy tent in Glasgow, Scotland, on the 31st of December, 1893, and lived the life of a traveling gypsy fortune-teller until sixteen years of age," said another newspaper splash in the lead-up to the 1926 camp meeting.[41] Converted at sixteen, Gypsy Pat Smith was driven away by his father, started preaching but stopped when World War I took place. He enlisted and was among the first British troops to enter France.[42] Later promoted to captain, he was wounded twice at the Battle of the Somme and hospitalized for nineteen months but refused discharge. Again, it was easy to get the evangelists confused, especially since Rodney Gypsy Smith, sometimes identified as "Gipsey," as was Capt. Gypsy Pat Smith, was also born in a Romani tent, only near London, England, in 1860. He too was converted at age sixteen. Of his life it was also said "his family history reads like a romance."[43] Yes, Capt. Gypsy Pat Smith soldiered in World War I, but Rodney Gypsey Smith visited British troops in France during the war for the YMCA. Thus, he too could address religious gatherings on topics such as "Just Behind the Firing Line in France."[44] Both Romani evangelists liked to sing. Rodney Gypsy Smith would stop preaching and break into song; Capt. Gypsy Pat Smith was known for his tenor voice and for directing his own choir.[45] One can't help but wonder how many campers at the Marengo County Union Camp in 1926 and 1927 were confused as to the identity of the "Gypsy Smith" preaching to them or, at the very least, confused by some of the details of lives that were virtually parallel at points. Actually, newspaper reporting on the various Gypsy Smiths wasn't always clear, so it isn't remarkable that camp-meeting attendees might get confused. As one newspaper put it in a not all that helpful way, "The evangelist is one of the two original Gypsy Smiths, born in a gypsy camp and later entering the evangelistic field."[46] That description was applied to British Rodney Gypsy Smith, who was holding a tent revival in the city park in Decatur, Alabama.

Likewise, it was Rodney Gypsy Smith whose name was pulled into a squabble over a proposed auditorium issue in Birmingham.[47] The renowned British evangelist couldn't accept an invitation to visit because "'certain conditions which prevail,' a sufficient spirit of co-operation among the pastors, to further the proposition to build an auditorium, was not present, the Birmingham Pastors union passed a resolution . . . dissolving all auditorium committees which have been appointed and dropping the entire matter." The fly in the ointment, according to the pastor of the Woodlawn Methodist Church, was Frank P. Glass, editor of the *Birmingham News* and chairman of the building committee. Then, two years later, the "Gypsy Smith Auditorium Company" was announced, to be organized with $10,000 in capital stock to pay Rodney Gypsy Smith's expenses in holding a fall revival.[48]

But it was Gypsy Smith Jr. who objected to his name being pulled into a political brouhaha in a Savannah, Georgia, mayoral race.[49] He had conducted a revival in Savannah in October 1922, and now sought to extricate his name from politics: "I came to Savannah with only one message; that was that the people of Savannah would become reconciled to God through Jesus Christ." He never preached anything related to local politics, he said. And it was Gypsy Jr. who came to Selma in 1929 at the behest of the city's spiritual leaders to confront the "appallingly indifferent and callous" hearts of "church folk."[50] A Baptist layman on the evangelism committee sought to counter a rumor that Gypsy Jr. had been guaranteed a set amount of money beforehand rather than the agreed-upon expenses incurred. It was the kind of worldly obstacle—the rumor—that was holding back support for the revival, the Baptist layman said.

But it wasn't either the father or son evangelist that caused a controversy in Philadelphia regarding American troops. No, that was Capt. Gypsy Pat Smith, charged in the press with willingness to "sacrifice the truth to a desire for notoriety."[51] It seems that while speaking at a Presbyterian Ministerial Association in the city, Gypsy Pat questioned the fighting spirit and experience of American soldiers when compared to troops from Great Britain and other countries, the latter "brought into touch with God and eternity by four years of grim warfare." It wasn't the kind of press you wanted your name mistakenly associated with if you were Gypsy Smith Sr. or Gypsy Smith Jr., particularly in light of the blood-boiling outrage the comment sparked among veterans. If anything, that only went double when divorce and allegations of sexual impropriety was concerned. Now, the newspapers tried to separate the three evangelists for clear understanding by all.

In Tuscaloosa, a letter to the editor in the summer of 1927, just before Gypsy Pat Smith was scheduled to make a return appearance in Dixons Mill, read:

> A statement has been going the rounds in the papers to the effect that Mrs. Gypsy Smith, Jr., is suing her husband for divorce. Since

> Gypsy, Jr., held a meeting here some two years ago and since therefore our people are greatly interested I beg your indulgence.
>
> The reference is not to Gypsy Smith, Jr., nor to his honored father, Gypsy Smith, Sr., but is said to be regarding one who calls himself Gypsy 'Pat' Smith and who is no relation whatever to the Smiths mentioned above."[52]

The letter writer noted that Gypsy Sr. lived in Cambridge, England, and, despite his many trips to America, had never owned a home in the United States. Gypsy Jr. owned a home in Noank, Connecticut, not on Contentment Island, where, ironically enough, the "Gypsy" who was involved in the divorce lived. For Mrs. Gypsy Smith Jr., happily married, the confusion of names was said to have "caused a great deal of embarrassment." Other Alabama newspapers tried to set the record straight about which Gypsy Smith was getting divorced but only added to the confusion. One cited "Gypsy Pat Smith, Jr." as the name of the marriage-challenged evangelist and quipped, "The real Gypsy, Jr., is pleasantly remembered in Montgomery. His friends are thinking of voting to rechristen this Gypsy Pat Smith, Jr. He should be content with the good old name of Pat since there are two other Gypsy Smiths, both well behaved."[53] Within a few weeks, another state newspaper added more scandalous details: Capt. Gypsy Pat Smith accused his wife of "cruelty and infidelity"; that the evangelist had been in a sanitarium for several weeks; that Mrs. Smith in a countersuit charged her husband with unfaithfulness and cruelty.[54] The child both parties sought custody of was identified as "'Gypsy' Pat Smith, Jr.," which no doubt added to the existing confusion of names.

Certainly, if emerging details of Gypsy Pat Smith's life looked bad in Alabama, on the ground in Connecticut, where these details were more granular, the view was infinitely worse. Up there it was said that the man who had converted thousands of people couldn't keep the peace with his wife; that his "creed" failed him.[55] The Gypsy Pat Smith creed was summarized in 10 words: Sincerity, Smile, Winsomeness, Love, Truth, Humility, Loyalty, Stickability, Push, and Optimism. "Love" in his credo was his oft-repeated maxim, "For love begets love; like begets like; hate begets hate." Connecticut newspapers cataloged

Figure 10. This depiction of English evangelist Rodney Gypsy Smith ran in the January 7, 1909, issue of the *Marion County News*. Figuring out which Gypsy Smith was which was problematic in those days.

the sobering, spirit-killing details. How Gypsy Pat, described as a "famous preacher of tolerance," evicted his wife of seven years from the house they lived in on Contentment Island. How she and their fifteen-month-old son were forced to live with friends in Stamford, Connecticut. How Karin Tjader Smith said she was "tired of it all" and her evangelist husband said he'd torn up all her photographs. How, following their marriage in 1920, Mrs. Smith had bought a piece of property on Contentment Island Road, only Gypsy Pat said he bought the property in her name. How a "gorgeous home" was eventually built on the property, but, in the newspaper's words, "There was hardly peace in the house of Contentment Island Road from almost the very beginning." How Gypsy Pat on May 27, 1927, told his wife he was ill, had no will, and wanted to straighten out legal matters so as not to leave her with problems; would she deed the property to him? How she signed the deed, realized almost immediately that she'd made a mistake, asked Gypsy Pat to undo it, but, in her words, he ordered her out of the house and "boasted of packing two guns" in the process. How a few days later Gypsy Pat entered a Connecticut sanitarium suffering from an overdose of medicine ("poison" in some reporting) and had attempted suicide. How Gypsy Pat said his wife left him without reason. How Mrs. Smith's friends said Gypsy Pat wasn't physically cruel to her but was "intolerably mean" in other ways and wasn't all he appeared to be when standing behind a pulpit at one of his religious rallies across the United States. How Gyspy Pat said, "Of course I will continue my preaching . . . A man cannot be blamed for something his wife has done."

The couple countersued each other. Both said the other had been unfaithful and claimed "intolerable cruelty."[56] Mrs. Smith said that between the date of their marriage and up to the date her husband evicted her from their home on Contentment Island, Gypsy Pat had committed adultery with one Jane Stiles and other women and that he had what was described as a "permanent and incurable disease" he had never told her about.[57] Asked where her husband was, Mrs. Smith said she didn't know. The reporting was that he had not only been in a sanitarium, but that he had just left for Alabama, which presumably meant Dixons Mill.[58] In the summer of 1928, Gypsy Pat Smith's wife was granted a divorce, but the findings of the court regarding the allegations on both sides were never made public.[59] Perhaps that was because, right from the start, it was said regarding a court fight between the famous evangelist and his wife, "The revelations . . . may rock New York and Connecticut society to its very foundations."[60]

From all indications, nothing about the scandal in Connecticut rocked the Marengo County Camp Meeting in 1927 when Gypsy Pat Smith returned. Behind him in Connecticut was a veritable plague of damning facts, allegations, and innuendo. The details including divorce, infidelity, cruelty, a threat involving guns, a suicide attempt, financial miscarriages, some kind of mystery ailment or incurable disease related to the "flesh," and the difficulty of reconciling the war hero and converted Gypsy who'd preached to tens of thousands and saved thousands of souls with the mean, shady character living on Contentment Island. None of it apparently mattered in Alabama, since Gypsy Pat Smith picked up right where he left off in 1926, namely, drawing eight to ten thousand people to hear him deliver three addresses on opening day of the camp meeting.[61] State reporting on Gypsy Pat's divorce by some state newspapers did nothing to affect the crowd's size or blunt its enthusiasm, not even when the "Gipsey" Smith "widely known in Alabama and Mississippi"—presumably Gypsy Smith Jr., son of the British evangelist—stated at the time the camp meeting started that he had no connection to Gypsy Pat Smith.[62] Speaking of matters crying out for reconciliation, US Congressman John McDuffie of Alabama, a featured speaker at the camp meeting in 1927, was reported to have said that the "old time religion was the hope of the country" and that the Dixons Mill camp meeting was one of Alabama's great institutions.[63] Juxtapose that with the scuttlebutt swirling around in Connecticut at the same time, how the "differences" that ultimately led to the divorce of Gypsy Pat Smith and his wife, Karin, started in 1926 on just the kind of spiritual trek Gypsy Pat was on at the moment in Dixons Mill: an evangelistic tour in New Zealand during which Karin, "in ill health, and much against her will," accompanied her husband.[64] It's hard to imagine the crowd at the Dixons Mill camp meeting being able to cope with any insinuation that anything connected with the sacred camp-meeting experience could lead to home wrecking, especially the home of the bright evangelistic star lecturing them on spiritual matters; that he could be involved in something as worldly as a property dispute might have seemed unthinkable to the thousands who turned out to hear him.[65]

We can only speculate as to why the camp meeting played out the way it did in 1927, with campers apparently unaware of, or paying no attention to, the reality that unfolded in Connecticut. When the 1926 camp meeting had ended, during which Gypsy Pat's "masterful sermons attracted great crowds in spite of adverse weather conditions," it was noted that the evangelist had agreed to come back in 1927 and bring his wife and child with him.[66] Maybe campers didn't read the scattered state reporting on Gypsy Pat Smith's divorce and its shocking details. Maybe it had something to do with the confusion of names that plagued reporting on too many "Gypsy Smiths." Perhaps the most shocking example of confusion over the three "Gypsy" men occurred in none other than *Time* magazine when it reported in 1928 this litany of mistakes: "Divorced. Rodney ('Gypsy') Smith, famed evangelist; by Karin Tjader Smith; in Bridgeport, Conn. She charged "intolerable" cruelty after having been persuaded to withdraw worse charges. Born in a gypsy camp in Scotland, Rodney Smith found God in the Salvation Army, in London, when he was 17. Since then, for 50 years, he has preached and sung all over the world."[67] A couple of weeks later the editors at *Time* were notified of the mistaken identity by one "Henry S. Coffin":

> Sir:
>
> In your issue of July 2 . . . you have unintentionally confused the internationally known evangelist "Gypsy" Smith . . . with a much younger man, Captain "Gypsy Pat" Smith. . . . This younger man of Gypsy origin after the War became an itinerant preacher, and, to the regret of "Gypsy" Smith, took that word as part of his public name. There is no kinship whatever between the two men. It is bad enough that his unhappy marital affairs should bring into disrepute this younger man's rather crude religious efforts; but let not his collapse reflect upon a Christian preacher who for years has rendered blameless service to churches in many lands.[68]

The letter writer was Henry Sloane Coffin, president of Union Theological Seminary in New York, one of the most prominent Presbyterian ministers in the United States. If *Time* could mix-up evangelists and have to be gently scolded by a prominent divine, certainly Alabama campers could be confused by a trinity of Gypsy Smiths. When the 1925 camp meeting in Dixons Mill concluded, it was reported how efforts were underway "to secure the noted evangelist Gypsy Smith for the 1926 camp meeting."[69] Not Gypsy Smith Sr. or Jr. or Gypsy Pat—just Gypsy Smith, as if there was but one. Maybe the campers didn't know there were so many and that was confusing. Or, if they knew, maybe the campers just didn't care that Gypsy Pat Smith had clay feet; maybe they were in the grips of a group contagion like the one that once jerked believers back and forth like a sapling in a cyclone—something that defied explanation! Maybe it had something to do with the camp meeting's religious fervor waning; the fever of sin cooling as the camp meeting became more Chautauqua-like, more diffused.

At times twentieth-century camp meetings sounded like those of old: "The Alabama Conference of Seventh-Day Adventists has just held its annual camp meeting in the beautiful grove in north Clanton owned by Mr. F. A. Gulledge of Verbena. Nearly forty tents were pitched in the grove. A large pavilion in which most of the public services were held occupied the front portion of the grounds. There were separate tents for the young people and children, also a large dining tent where splendid meals were served three times a day on the cafeteria plan."[70] Sure, maybe the Clanton campground had electricity and water supplied by the "Clanton electric plant and waterworks," but the "family tents" occupied by people from all over the state, the "warm, hearty handshakes" and fraternal and cooperative spirit, well, those were what made for successful camp meetings a hundred years before as surely as they did in 1921. The raw politics that came out of the 1921 camp meeting in Clanton, however, didn't smack of anything associated with the raw spirit of Cane Ridge—perhaps after Cane Ridge, certainly. The camp meeting produced a resolution regarding "Religious Liberty":

> WHEREAS, There is a nation wide [*sic*] effort being put forth by certain religious organizations to Puritanize America, and to revive the Sunday 'blue laws' of Colonial times when the church and state were united, therefore be it
>
> RESOLVED, That we, the members of the Alabama Conference of

> Seventh-Day Adventists, in mass meeting assembled at the camp meeting at Clanton, September 1–11, do hereby petition the United States Congress not to pass any of the pending compulsory Sunday observance bills. We are opposed to the Sunday "Blue laws" because they are religious in character and contrary to the genius of America in system of government, in violation of the American principle of the separation of church and state, destructive of the First Amendment of the Federal Constitution, opposed to the best interests of both church and state, and above all they are manifestly un-American, un-Christian, un-Constitutional, parital, and a piece of legislation, favoring certain sects and discounting others under duress of civil law.

If that could be considered a break with the spiritual tradition of early camp meetings, keep in mind it didn't happen all at once, nor were the Seventh-Day Adventists the only ones using the camp meeting in such a way. After all, Dr. W. C. Blasingame of Montgomery was on hand with Gypsy Pat Smith in Dixons Mill in 1927 to lecture campers who were interested on "Better Health Conditions in Alabama."[71] Long before the Baptists turned Shocco Springs into a resort and conference center, they used campgrounds in Dixons Mill and Bluff Springs to promote denominational business. "Some things which Baptists are doing," was a discussion at Bluff Springs in 1910, which sounded like something that would have been part of a slide-show presentation a few years later.[72] At Dixons Mill, Baptists used the campground as a training school meeting for Sunday School workers: "Rev. Bob Jones, of Montgomery, the famous Methodist evangelist, whose field has for several years extended beyond the limit of his own denomination, and who is said to have conducted evangelistic campaigns in 30 states, will be another speaker."[73] That's the Bob Jones from the introduction, the other luminary, like Gypsy Pat Smith, who preached more than once at Dixons Mill. Within a few years the Methodists and Baptists would be sending out a warning to avoid the Reverend Jones. They argued that he was a threat to local churches and a spiritual grifter fleecing flocks to the advantage of no one but Bob Jones. Whatever conjecture we come up with to explain what happened over time to the institution of the camp meeting, whatever theory we put forward, must of necessity be multifaceted. We can immediately dismiss any pious musing about how the world eventually crept into the sacred idea of camping since the world was present from the beginning.

# 3

## "Of Course the Devil Was There—He Always Goes to Camp Meetings"

The report in 1883, that the Kentucky Methodist Conference was of the opinion that there was too much of the world and worldliness in some camp meetings, would have evoked a hearty amen from brothers and sisters in Alabama.[1] Even at that late date they were trying to escape to the wilderness; trying to get far enough away that the world wouldn't interfere with their devotions. "The annual camp-meeting of the Eufaula district commenced at Wilkie's Spring, in Barbour county, last Friday, and continued until to-day. This camp-meeting is probably one of the best managed open-air meetings in the country, and, by reason of its remote location among the sequestered shades of Mt. Andrew, in Barbour county, some distance from any large city or railroad town, the devotions of the pious Methodists are not disturbed by the train-loads of sacrilegious excursionists, whose presence at a modern camp-meeting is almost as fatal to peace and order as the dragoons of Claverhouse were at the interdicted gatherings of the courageous Scotch covenanters."[2] The same was said of Little Texas camp ground in East Alabama, "about fifteen miles (coon skin measure), South of Auburn, and about that distance from every where [*sic*] else. . . . When those wise headed ones who had the location of Texas camp ground under consideration, no doubt other more convenient places were in nomination, and received due consideration, but they thought they would place it so far away in the pine woods and great thoroughfare of travel, that the Devil would not molest, nor make them afraid, but they found out since then, that the Devil goes where ever men and women go."[3] It seemed the Devil could bedevil a camp meeting perpetually or do away with one before it became a tradition in a community. Regarding the latter, the story was told of a short-lived camp meeting on Big Creek in Dale County that started around 1850 but was plagued by "a lot of rowdy fellows" who got up a horse race near the camp. One of the rowdies was killed, and that put an end to the Watford camp meeting.[4] There were other camp meetings that quickly flamed out around Ozark and Dale counties. "As early as 1841 and continuing for three years a camp meeting was organized and held at Zion Church, three miles southeast of Haw Ridge. Some persons 'without the fear of God or the law of the land before their eyes,['] disturbed the people who had met for worship. They were arrested and brought before Reverend Levi Dowling, a local preacher, and a justice of the peace, who bound them over to the County Court, of which Gappa G. Yelberton presided. He convicted them and fined each of them twenty-five dollars." What was described as the "lawless element" also inserted itself among the devout around 1846 at the "Chitty Camp Ground, at Bethel Church, nine miles east of Ozark," where their disruptive influence resulted in a story being told by one of the camp-meeting leaders that doubtlessly would have echoed in response across the state by campers, "It is so!" It seems that when God made people of clay, he leaned them against trees to dry, but some of them fell over and "scrambled off" before any brains were placed in their heads. "Presiding Elder Armstrong," who told the story, claimed to see the descendants of those brainless ones right there in the campground. For them, the camp meeting was a "religious carnival."[5] "The interest of every one [*sic*] in the neighborhood and its vicinity was aroused and excited. It mattered not whether they were saints or sinners, whether they considered themselves as of the elect or the unregenerate, they were all interested alike. The elect attended to pray for the welfare of the non-elect, and for spiritual strengthening and refreshment for church and individual; and the unregenerate went to be amused, possibly benefited, and because everybody else would be sure to be there."

Yes, writer Eben E. Rexford's 1900 assessment of the camp meeting appeared in serialized fiction in newspapers, but what he said was factual, actual news of the day:

> Senator Ware . . . offered a bill to prohibit the sale of liquors within five miles of any religious camp-meetings in Choctaw, Clarke and Washington counties.[6]

> On motion of Mr. Walton, Senate reconsidered the vote passing bill forbidding sale of liquor within 3 miles of Smith's Camp Ground in Choctaw Co. An amendment was adopted and bill passed.[7]

> H.B. 451. To preserve order and to prohibit the carrying on or engaging in any secular business for profit within one mile of Choctaw Camp Ground, and Camp Springs Camp in Choctaw county, during the time that camp meetings are held for conducting religious worship. Passed.[8]

> To preserve order at the Cold Water Camp Grounds in Clay county, and at Unity Camp Grounds in Pickens county.[9]

The following appeared under "The Legislature" in a single issue of a newspaper:

> — To prohibit sale of liquor in one mile of Wilkie Camp Grounds, Barbour county.
> — To preserve order at Choctaw Camp Ground & Camp Springs Camp Ground in Choctaw County.
> — To preserve order at the Asbury camp ground in Monroe county, at Spring Hill camp ground, Butler county, at Potterville camp ground and Ramage Springs camp ground, Pike county, and at Tabernacle and Andrews' Chapel camp ground, Pickens county.
> — To preserve order at the Sims Camp Grounds in the county of Randolph.[10]

If morals could be legislated, Alabama politicians would have done so on behalf of religious camp meetings during the nineteenth century. Needless to say, it wasn't to be. Somebody named "Old Tubbs" wrote a letter to the editor in 1884 concerning a pleasant Sunday he spent at Peniel Baptist Church in Clarke County, "a congregation of fine looking young ladies and proud mothers, with fat pretty babies, and splendid, healthy looking men, it has not been my pleasure to meet in a long time."[11] "It reminded me of the old camp-meetings, when I was a boy, minus the tents, hidden bottles and demijohns of 'tangle-leg.' [*sic*] The time, I doubt not, is rapidly approaching when the bloated face, red nose and uncouth manner of the inebriate will be a thing of the past. God hasten the time when, by common consent and good legislation, the great enemy of society and good morals will be eradicated from our country." A prophet Old Tubbs wasn't. The inebriate, red nose and all, with his loud and boisterous ways was a hard fellow to bring to contrition, let alone eradicate; nevertheless, hope sprang eternal with each camping season. At Little Texas it was hoped the camp-meeting managers would do a better job than they had in keeping order.[12] When the "colored Methodists of Union Springs District" camped at Chunnenuggee Ridge in Bullock County, the presiding elder made the rules clear: no selling of refreshments; the camp-meeting committee would handle the entertaining; and "proper decorum" was expected under the law.[13] That was echoed nearly thirty years later at the Pea River camp meeting: "No cold drink or other stands will be allowed on or near the grounds, which will be thoroughly policed" and "No rowdyism or undue behavior will be permitted."[14] At Douglasville in Escambia County, they referred to such behavior as "tents of distraction" that were to be kept out of the camp ground.[15] One has to wonder if Mr. J. J. Padgett's "two story public tent" at Little Texas camp meeting qualified as a "tent of distraction" at Douglasville. William George in his letter to the editor said he could vouch for the fact that Padgett's table was "supplied with the best the market affords."[16] Indeed, Padgett's table had everything needed by campers and horses alike and was reason in itself for everybody to go to camp meeting. According to William George, "Some there are who oppose camp meetings on general principles. This is not strange, since we find some one or more oppose everything under the sun. I can see no reason why people may not assemble themselves together at any time and place for civil and social purpose and more especially when the chief object is to pay vows to the Most High, under the eye of the church. True, some imprudent things may be done by imprudent persons, but such would be more likely to happen under other circumstances." Likewise, somebody at the county seat weekly in Butler County, not that far from the Florida line, could understand the business side to the camp meeting. The newspaper's boss was attending the camp meeting in Bogia, Florida, and the faithful employee said, "We trust that he will, mingling religion with business, come back with a large list of subscribers to the best weekly in Alabama."[17] Still, not everybody was as broad-minded as William George or the newspaper wag. Not everybody could tolerate the world and church pitching tents so close to each other. Okay, horses were understandable: people wanted and needed their stock to be taken care of while they tented for the Lord, and the prices should be fair. That's why the Union Church camp meeting in Clarke County allowed for a public lot on the campgrounds for stock—preachers' horses were taken care of at no cost.[18] But that was the extent of the commercialism. "We do not expect any other money-making machine, of any shape or form, on the camp-ground, and hope that no one will attempt to carry anything there that will have a tendency to defeat the object of the meeting. A police will be appointed to keep order on the ground." An act by the state legislature to incorporate the campgrounds at Unity Grove was done so to keep order and keep down disturbances, as was the election of a camp marshal.[19] For some, the camp meeting was, sadly enough, the antithesis of Godly conduct and deportment: "Prepare to celebrate Christmas this year in the service of God instead of 'on a high,' as you have been used to doing. So many people fail to remember that occasion is to celebrate the birth of Christ, and should not be turned into a camp meeting for the devil. Ponder over this and do your duty."[20]

Sometimes a camp meeting's success was measured in terms of law and order, so to speak. Again, Little Texas and Unity Grove provide examples, respectively:

> The crowd to-day is not so large as usual, but quite an orderly assemblage. The only trouble the police force experiences is in trying to make one attend services at the arbor. A few sometimes prefer to sit in front of their tents while preaching is going on, which conduct

is expressly forbidden by law. This, however, is not at all general and there results no evil there-from.[21]

It is worthy of record that for so large a number of people gathered together a whole week the order and behavior exceeded the general expectation. Several visitors, being pleased with the camp-ground and its prospects as a means of doing good, have resolved to obtain lots, and build tents next year.[22]

The camp meeting [at Choctaw camp ground] was the most quiet and orderly affair of the kind we have ever attended.[23]

The tenter in Choctaw County, who saw morals "'in a high state of cultivation,' and rapidly advancing toward a point beautiful to behold," attributed the ascendancy to a tandem effort, namely, "The children of God and the friends of law and order, have just closed the 'Oaktuppa Camp Meerting,' held at Bethel church, four miles Northeast of Isney. There were thirteen good wooden tents and twenty-one tenters, besides many canvas tents that whitened the surrounding hill tops. On Sabbath the attendance was estimated at 1200."[24]

Still, even if you could find enough "wilderness" to escape to, put the rowdies on notice, cut out the wrong kind of "spirit"-filled camper, and weed out those trying to make a buck or getting elected to political office, the religious camp meeting remained an uneasy spiritual event. Instances abounded where weather was cited as the culprit that cut down on the harvest of souls. Rain was understandable, but in 1886 it was "clouds of dust" that blunted the attendance at the Spring Hill camp meeting near Greenville in Bulter County.[25] Also, a successful camp meeting meant having the right preachers, preferably "orators" campers had heard of:

Thursday, the second day, there were in attendance not over 175 people, including ladies, reported a gentleman to the TIMES. On that day the audience was addressed by Mr. Gilley, Mr. Lightner and Mr. Huggins. The same gentlemen, we believe, addressed the meeting the day before.

> It does not appear to have amounted to much, this camp-meeting. The famous orators advertised did not materialize and the meeting had to put up with addresses from gentlemen unknown to fame.[26]

Fame had its place, which explains why camp meetings like the one in Dixons Mill had evangelists such as Gypsy Pat Smith and Bob Jones Sr., flamboyant preachers with riveting personal stories, as in Gypsy Pat's gypsy background, or rollicking reputations, such as Bob Jones Sr.'s for giving the saloon industry a black eye.[27] Also, a good dose of fear or an anti-God threat was bound to draw a crowd, as it did in 1925 for Dr. Fritz Rauschenberg's address on evolution.[28]

Even good weather and famous preachers couldn't guarantee heaven on earth during a week or two of encampment. Horses could cause problems, again. At a Mt. Andrew camp meeting in Barbour County, some horses died for different reasons, leaving one young man who'd borrowed his employer's horse to seek a cheap replacement.[29] A young woman, "Miss Mary Wilson," from Butler in Choctaw County was injured returning from camp meeting when the team attached to the wagon in which she and other young women were riding acted up, and she jumped.[30] Horse thieves helped themselves to some animals at "Asberry" (Asbury) camp meeting in Monroe County.[31] In neighboring Clarke County, it was reported that four well-armed thieves, riding three mules and a horse without saddles, passed through Choctaw Corner (northwestern Clarke County).[32] There they were overtaken, "broiling some beef for supper, having killed a cow a short distance from where they were found." The thieves fled leaving the stolen animals behind. Nobody wanted to claim ownership of scoundrels who'd stoop so low to steal from Christians encamped for the Lord. A Wilcox County weekly claimed the scurrilous four were from Clarke County, so the Clarke weekly set things straight: they were from Marengo County![33] Yes, the horse thieves had "emigrated to Texas" some years before, but now the newspaper pronounced the four scalawags in words that might have come from a brush arbor: they were men of "no continuing city." A couple of years after the visitation by horse thieves, Asbury camp meeting again suffered an unfortunate event. After tents were pitched, straw and trash were gathered for burning, but a spark the following day set a tent on fire that spread and resulted in forty-six tents burning.[34] "The camp meeting will be held in spite of the disaster," it was reported. How the campers understood the tragedy—an act of God or something else—is anybody's guess.

The camp-meeting experience involved drunkenness, rowdyism, worldliness, and godlessness, not by choice but necessity. Likewise, it couldn't avoid issues that overflowed into religion: evolution, prohibition, and the perils of progress to name a few. Camp-meeting evangelists fearlessly stormed the walls that kept sinners separated from God and sought to break the barriers down and liberate the captives. There were, however, instances when the preaching of the gospel seemed to drip with faint-heartedness from the lips of God's warriors, who avoided certain subjects the way water flows around a stone. Perhaps the timidity was more cultural than anything—a sign of the times, not so much the uncomfortable proof that the world wasn't deterred by the American wilderness or, later on, by some grove of trees or thatch of woodland. It was more that human nature was always packed and ready to travel, even to a camp meeting. That's the reason in 1885 that "VIATOR" wrote how young people would never go along with abolishing the camp meeting due to what transpired in the tents and under the oaks, namely, unwritten romances.[35] Not everybody at the camp meeting was looking to benefit their soul; some were nothing more than picnickers whose desires lay elsewhere,[36] much as did the two bird dogs jockeying for position beside the pretty penitent kneeling at the altar.[37] There was a lot of innuendo:

> —The Misses Dalton, of Eufaula, are visiting the family of Rev. B. C. Bennett, near Pea River and attending the Ramage Springs camp meeting. They captured the hearts of several noble young Trojans, all of whom expect to visit Eufaula soon on a delicate mission.[38]

> Mr. C. I. Hendrix and Miss Gloe Barber, living in south Choctaw, were married at Quitman Monday of last week. The courtship of this matrimonial alliance is said to have terminated at Frost's Bridge camp-meeting, as did also the union of several other couples who recently sacrificed themselves at Hymen's altar.[39]

Even in 1953, when the camp meeting was barely holding on in Alabama, it was recalled from the perspective of the good old days: "Camp meetings were and are a peculiarly Southern institution. In the days when travel was difficult and neighbors were distant, camp meetings had their social as well as religious aspects. Thousands gathered at the camp grounds to spend the week, seeking primarily the gospel of Christ. The religious side would always be the first order of the week's meeting but many a young couple paired off for life after a week's chaperoned courtship in the shadow of the old camp grounds."[40] Chaperoned? That young couples were always escorted seems as unlikely as the camp meeting ever getting rid of the "tangle-leg" or "oysters" that enticed a certain segment to tent; you know, the "Johnnie High" the Reverend Fendley mentioned. As for the social aspect of the camp meeting, while there's no denying it provided a much needed outlet in that regard for folk scattered across the wilderness, don't be fooled by the seemingly mild-mannered term "social." Elder William Ashcraft, a well-known Baptist preacher, wasn't. It was one of the five points he made in the years immediately after the American Civil War in a "circular letter" regarding a certain "popular amusement," namely, dancing, and the evils thereof.[41] There was a physical component in dancing—as well as intellectual, social; moral, and spiritual aspects in it, according to Elder Ashcraft.

*Physical.* "Dancing is, really, a physical exercise, too violent to be healthful; it is exceedingly dangerous. To those who are in the habit of taking exercise, it is that much more than they need. To those who take none, it is exhausting. It is very exciting.—And the excitement connected with it is purely animal, while the enjoyment is carnal in its nature and tendency." When the Bible urged praising God's name in the dance, well, that was a sacred dance, unlike the "mirthful amusements of the present day"—music and dance—"*artfully designed* to arouse the baser passions and feelings of our nature, and cause us to think only of the enjoyment of sensual pleasure for the present moment." Dance could intoxicate "our better feelings," impair judgment, and lead dancers into riotous behavior, even "instant death." Yes, death! Dancers, in crowded rooms, their bellies full of rich food and strong drink, shut off from fresh air, out at night when nature called for rest and sleep, the ladies "dressed more thinly and tightly than usual" go rushing out into the cold night air, well, it could weaken the system.

*Intellectual.* Dancing suppressed intellectual pursuits. Dancing placed a higher value on "gait and gestures, peculiar to the ball room, than upon intellectual excellence." Whatever suppresses the intellect to advance "sensual gratification" is a perversion.

*Social.* "Gadding about" is a bad habit. "Debating, Reading and Singing societies should be formed for the benefit and entertainment of all." Every community needed a library . . . and if not, then the art of conversation should be advanced. You can't carry on a conversation while dancing, so dancing is a "Social Evil."

*Moral.* What possible harm could come of dancing? Well, "feasting, the revelling, the evil company, the evil thoughts, the forgetfulness of God"—those for a start. Without those things, who's going to a ballroom? Dancing is all about carnal pleasure!

*Spiritual.* Dancing is nothing more than preparation for "vice and sin." "No one ever yet saw a pious dancer."

Elder Ashcraft was clearly aware of the existence of carnal pleasure, sensual gratification, and how humans' animal nature was easily aroused by the "most thrilling emotions." Yet, the sexes mingled at the camp meeting, stirred by ecstatic movements of the Holy Spirit and experiencing collective ecstasy; they hugged, danced, and laughed, but these actions resulted not in condemnation but word bouquets regarding Hymen's altar, captured hearts, unwritten romances and courtships. About as *un*spiritual as it got in Alabama in talking about the sexes tenting together seems to have been male banter, such as this: "When a Choctaw county woman gets into her cranium the idea of going to camp meeting she can, thoroughly unaided, contrive more means of transportation in one hour than would occur to the mind of her husband (or sweetheart, as the case may be) in a life time. If you want to witness an exhibition of feminine temper that is simply awful, just balk one of these angelic creatures in her efforts to attend camp meeting. We speak by the card."[42] That was merely a fun-loving sentiment in the nineteenth-century version of the battle of the sexes. But what about all the talking-points Elder Ashcraft laid out in his circular letter regarding the carnality of dance? Did that apply only to worldly ballrooms, or could it equally apply to embraces at the brush arbor and holy kisses and swooning in each other's arms as the Holy Spirit moved over the campsite the way the Death Angel did when it passed over the Egyptians, slaying left and right? Letter writer William George was aware of "imprudent things" and "imprudent persons" within the camp, so why so much timidity in calling out sex?

Regarding that, consider a chain of events from 1885. A newspaper correspondent wrote about a "sad scene" encountered on the Montgomery & Eufaula Railroad, where a "deserted wife, with five children" was riding the train.[43] The children ranged in age from infancy to nine, and the woman, with a ticket to Macon, Georgia, didn't have the means to reach Brunswick, Georgia, where she had friends. The train conductor, appealing to passengers, raised eleven dollars to help the woman and children. According to Mrs. J. W. Wesley, she was a "deserted wife," her husband having run off six months earlier with a widow, one Mrs. Mattie Mastress. The beleaguered woman, who had lived the last ten years near Georgiana in Butler County, had reason to believe that the philanderer and his paramour were now in north Alabama. The correspondent, throwing away any semblance of journalistic objectivity, fired off this line: "Her recreant husband should be out in the coal mines and made to support his helpless family."

Hold your horses! said J. R. Stott, in a letter from Georgiana dated September 19 and appearing in the same publication next day, the letter addressed to "EDITORS ADVERTISER."[44] Stott, who appears to have been a Georgiana businessman and justice of the peace, sought to correct the newspaper reporting on the deserted wife and her children. First, the Rev. J. W. Wesley came to the Georgiana area—was "assigned"—three years before and had the reputation of being a "Christian gentleman." Second, six months ago he and his wife separated, and the preacher had been living with a church member ever since. Third, that the preacher had "eloped" with Mattie Mastress or anyone else was false, as was the statement that Preacher Wesley was living in north Alabama. According to J. R. Stott, either Mrs. J. W. Wesley was lying or the newspaper correspondent had manufactured the story. The newspaper editor responded to J. R. Stott by noting the correspondent was "absolutely reliable."

The Stott letter prompted a response from the correspondent who initially reported on the sad case of the deserted woman and her children.[45] First, the correspondent defended the accuracy of the reporting by noting that the words Mrs. Wesley spoke were taken down as she spoke them. Second, there was no reason not to believe the woman; those who contributed money to help her and the children certainly believed her. Third, the woman didn't mention that the husband who abandoned her "was an alleged minister of the gospel." The correspondent learned that detail from J. R. Stott's letter. Lastly, if the correspondent was misled, so were the upstanding citizens of Montgomery, who were moved by the sad plight of the woman and children. In a matter of weeks another state publication weighed in on the sad case and, honestly, muddled it even more.[46] That newspaper concluded that the "same John" was being talked about in both cases: John, who abandoned a wife and five kids, and John, the reverend with the reputation of a Christian gentleman. The newspaper reached that conclusion by what it called "several circumstances," which are summarized here based on this author's best understanding of them with no claim to infallibility promoted in doing so.

John W. Wesley came to the Geneva-Dale counties area twenty-five years before with what was supposed to be his young wife, "where he lived a long while, professing conversion, joining the Church, becoming a Minister, and making many friends and enjoying considerable popularity as a comparatively uneducated, but seemingly earnest and energetic worker in the church."

Somewhere along the way an uncle of John's alleged wife, who had "some difference" with John, got even by telling how John had abandoned "a helpless wife in Georgia" and run off with the woman who was supposed to be his wife.

This caused John's church to confront him, and he confessed but explained it all by blaming it on the conduct of the wife he abandoned in Georgia.

With everything out in the open, either John Wesley divorced the wife in Georgia or she him, and he married the woman "with whom he had been living so long, in concubinage." Wouldn't that be the woman on the Montgomery & Eufaula train, the one with five kids? The one whom, apparently, ol' John had now abandoned and scooted off with Mattie Mastress or another woman?

If that interpretation is wrong, apologies to John W. Wesley, but the kernel or nugget to be noted for purposes here is the latter newspaper's conclusion: "The church . . . can carry without apparent detriment, Ministers who are educated too much, or not enough, who are too refined or too coarse, whose sermons and prayers are too long, or too short, or who talk through their nasal organs and the like; but it can not [*sic*] afford to carry a fellow who is the husband of more than one wife, and wherever one like that is found, pretending to minister in sacred things, his head should drop into the basket, without the benefit of clergy, and the sooner the better."

With such a sentiment duly noted in the secular media, why was it so hard to call out preachers and sex, especially when the two were connected? Drunks, horse-racing fools, tents of distraction occupied by materialists trying to make a buck, politicians corrupting the church with state-politicking, the curious lacking spiritual depth: all were duly recognized as camp-meeting stumbling blocks, but sex was treated with verbal brocades, while preachers compromised by the flesh largely went unscathed. Rev. John W. Wesley, no doubt guided by the Great Commission, simply moved on from allegations of multiple abandonments and concubinage to his next field, and forty years later Gypsy Pat Smith, his marriage in tatters, a named consort in the news, and ugly headlines involving everything the camp meeting was supposed to be against, returned to Dixons Mill to draw record crowds hungry for the gospel. Perhaps dealing head-on with preachers in the grip of the flesh would have been an admission already noted here, namely, that the camp meeting never escaped the world. If that was true, another issue the camp meeting failed to face heroically was one so ingrained in the culture and times that no amount of Christian discernment would suffice. Truthfully, no one even tried to hide it. You could see it across time, the tension involved: "We have heard severe comment passed upon the manner in which a protracted meeting (white) was conducted recently at Tompkinsville [Choctaw County]. Report has it, that a colored man present was invited to occupy a front seat and then requested to lead in singing, and that he was also called upon to pray. Several persons in attendance became very indignant."[47] Also, not far down on the page, this: "We hear that Rufus Doyle, a colored parson and one of the most consumate [*sic*] scoundrels in the county, has been sent to Kansas by the members of the 'Wesley M.E. Church' (col[ored]) near Mt. Sterling." Compare those to Gypsy Pat Smith in 1926 having "several hundred negroes . . . come and sing their spiritual songs,"[48] and, the following year, "A delightful feature of the evening's service was the singing of negro 'Spirituals' by Mrs. Bryant, nee Madelyn Sheppard, their plaintive melodes [*sic*], so expressive of the negro's religious experience were all compositions of the sweet singer."[49]

How the "negro's religious experience" was perceived from the sources was a hodge-podge to no surprise. Yes, newspapers carried notices of Black camp meetings: "There is to be another colored camp-meeting in this county—this time at Three Notch, commencing Friday, October 18th, and ending the 21st. This meeting is gotten up by the A.M.E. Zion people."[50] Yes, Black camp meetings had grifters too; at least, it was reported that way in the white press.

> —It is said that last Sunday a colored chevalier of industry collected ten cents from each camp-meeting pilgrim on the train from Troy, alleging that this was his bonus as charterer of the train. Marshal Dawson, on hearing of this little game, compelled him to refund his self-imposed toll-money. It was a bold racket.
>
> —A well-dressed negro man was arrested on one of the returning camp-meeting trains Sunday evening, charged with forging the name of J. L. Thomas to an order on L. Bernheimer, the amount being ten dollars. His name is W. W. Perry and he hails from Montgomery. The arrest was made by Marshal Dawson.

White press, maybe, but even Booker T. Washington, the renowned Black educator and author, saw problems in the Black camping experience. "The evils of camp meetings, excursions, etc., as usually conducted by the colored people" was just one topic of a Summer Assembly held in 1893 at Tuskegee Normal and Industrial Institute where Washington was president.[51]

And, yes, Black camp meetings had accidents and tragedies too.

"Gilbert, a nineteen-year-old colored boy of Spring Hill, fell under the cars of one of the camp-meeting trains, at the depot, Sunday morning, while the train was moving, and his left arm was crushed in such a manner as to necessitate immediate amputation. The forefinger of his right hand was also mashed off in the endeavor to secure his umbrella after his arm was mangled and while still under the cars." The white and Black camp meetings were alike in another way too.

> The A.M.E. missionary camp meeting is in progress. To-morrow there will be mixed services, and white people are specially invited.[52]

> The Altruists of Dora Baptist Sunday School entertained at a Poverty Social . . . The large crowd was divided into groups, and stunts formed a very amusing entertainment . . . The Negro Camp Meeting with Rev. T. F. Hendon as colored parson, was very laughable, and closed the stunts.[53]

Blacks could invite whites to camp meeting, but there was a lot less tension if the Blacks who came to the white religious gatherings were "black" in the sense of minstrel shows, that is, whites singing Black spirituals. A real "colored parson" might be deemed a scoundrel, but a white preacher (presumably in blackface) portraying a colored parson was good for a laugh. As time passed and the relevancy and efficacy of the camp meeting became subject of discussion, mocking commentary sometimes appeared:

> We have almost come to the conclusion that the day for camp meeting has past, and that there is more harm done at them than good; but when we hear the old gray headed veterans of the cross tell their experience, and in nearly every instance they tell about the camp meeting where they met the Lord and he spoke peace to their sin burdened souls, we begin to think we are wrong in being opposed to them, and also when we look round and see people, even members of the Methodist church there, who never hear preaching only at camp meeting then we withdraw all our opposition and say amen to them. We see some people go to camp meeting and get religion enough to last them

> the entire year. This is certainly a great advantage. No need of being a teacher in the Sunday School; no need of going to hear preaching every Sunday; no need of going to the Thursday night prayer meeting. What a vast amount of trouble this attending camp meeting once a year saves people.[54]

That sarcasm paled in comparison to a blunt-force "prayer" asking to be delivered "from ni**er camp meetings."[55]

The "'camp meeting' spell"—the "almost magic influence" that enthralled "almost every class and condition of humanity"—was said to involve elements of "faith, zeal, hospitality[,] gallantry and rascality." To that we add ungodly sex and godly racism.

# 4

## "Shun All Such Men as You Would a Viper"

When a book has gone through ten editions, somebody's done something right. When that book's title is *Crimes of Preachers in the United States and Canada*, however, it's obvious somebody has also done something wrong. When that tenth edition appeared in 1914, it was noted "the clergy have not ceased to furnish fresh material for its pages,"[1] hence the reason so many revisions of the book had occurred since its first appearance in 1881. That some Alabama ministers' names were included in the roll call of the scandalous and ignominious isn't as surprising as some of the theories advanced for preachers' bad behavior in general. Among the theories were the following: they had too much time to kill, spent in loafing and idleness (a theory voiced by a preacher!); they suffered from too much flattery and fawning; their preaching took so much out of a man that it led to a strain on his moral fiber; they were poorly paid; there was a bias against men of the cloth by businessmen; and they were easy targets for "yellow journalism." Even "a certain malignity in the constitution of the air" was cited, that said specifically regarding Kokomo, Indiana, where, over a six-month period in 1912, four scandals involving ministerial immorality took place. The air in Kokomo was "contraindicated for ministers," it was said, tongue-in-cheek. But there wasn't anything humorous for those whose names appeared in the ever-expanding register of preacher-criminals. They must have felt that the sun just wouldn't go down on their bad deeds, what with each new edition of the book. That's the way the Reverend Silas Williford, a Baptist in Geneva County,

Alabama, in 1891 might have felt. He is cited here for two reasons. For one, it was said he "*decamped* for parts unknown" when he, a fifty-year-old preacher with a wife and several children, ran off with another woman.[2] It wasn't as if he was at a camp meeting when he took off, but the newspaper that did the reporting used a root word that was well known in those days, one that unconsciously served notice, in a sense, that at any given moment all are merely "camping" on this earthly plane in spite of individual circumstances. The second reason Preacher Williford draws the short straw here is what was said about Dora Reddick, the other woman. She was identified as "a lewd woman who lived in the same neighborhood."

*Crimes of Preachers in the United States and Canada* was true to its word in transcribing its sad list straight from "the Original Newspapers" since the Reverend Williford's crime was recorded therein as "adultery, eloped with *lewd woman.*" Indeed, of all the preacher crime categories, a large number fell into those involving carnality and sex, a bewildering and overlapping sorting that included "Abortion and attempts to procure" (19 cases); "Adultery" (676); "Alienation of affections" (17); "Assault with intent to rape" (50); "Bastardy" (77); "Bigamy, attempted and accomplished" (144); "Debauchery" (52); "Enticing women and young girls" (15); "Immoralities with women and girls, miscellaneous and variously described" (223); "Rape in general" (43); "Seduction in general" (273); "Sodomy or unnatural crime" (67); "White slavery and pandering" (15).[3]

Again, while the camp meeting wasn't specifically correlated with any of the hellish crimes and criminal preachers, certainly these preachers' natural and unnatural proclivities were exhibited loud and clear through the crimes in the lists. That's what the following warning was: a kind of public safety bulletin, an Alabama heads-up. "We desire to say a few words of especial interest to those of our lady friends who read the NEWS. We want to tell you about a certain dangerous character, of whose existence many of you are entirely ignorant, although he can always be found in this as well as in every other community. He is seen daily in every city, town, village and hamlet throughout this broad land. We have frequently seen him at country churches, standing outside near the door—and at camp-meetings too."[4] This guy kind of slinked around ogling passing women and making "unregenerate, disrespectful remarks" about those he encountered. If you, young lady, missed coming under this guy's stare, "you are more fortunate than others of your sex. He generally takes his position in a conspicuous place—in front of a store or grocery door—and when a female passes by he is most sure to criticize her bustle or her pin back—and her foot, too, if she exposes it to view. But does he stop there? No. Nine times out of ten he will make use of some low-bred, vulgar remark, or unjust or ungentlemanly insinuation, that will be eagerly noted down by some third person who will repeat it to others, and they in turn will have to talk the matter over among confidential friends, who would not speak of it for the world, until it finally results in a foul, infamous slander, black enough to ruin for life the fair reputation of its unconscious victim and to damn its dastardly author forever." Like the red-faced, bloated drunk, this guy too "ought to be expelled from society, for they are a thousand times more to be dreaded than so many poisonous reptiles." Young men: don't listen to this snake or pass on any of his poison regarding a lady's character. Young ladies: this "contemptible puppy" will boast of "taking liberties" with the fairer sex, so, "Shun all such men as you would a viper."

A venom-spreading man, leering and lying in wait on the street corner or posted up with the no-accounts near a doorway where the ladies come and go; that was bad enough, but a snake in the grass at the camp meeting? What could be more unthinkable than a vipers' tangle passing for a human heart in one of the divines that allegedly came to camp meetings to save souls; what could be more unthinkable than a camp meeting, still within the historical era when the "Second Great Awakening" was shaping the contours of religion in America, having a connection to the grisly murder of a poor soul, sexual promiscuity, syphilis, aborting an unwanted pregnancy, or a denominational cover-up to boot?

It started in late 1832 in Rhode Island. The victim was a thirty-ish factory-worker named Sarah Maria Cornell. The person charged with her murder was Methodist minister Ephraim K. Avery from Bristol, Rhode Island. It was a historic murder, and it is mentioned here because the news of what occurred at a camp meeting reached all the way to Alabama and would be recalled periodically in the press for years to come. Why not? The camp meeting in the Northeast was not all that different from those in the South. A Connecticut notice of a camp meeting "at Simsbury, near the Farmington Canal," warned, "Pedlars [*sic*], and exhibitors of shows that may come to annoy the meeting, may expect to meet the rigor of the law."[5] That same year, 1830, in Massachusetts, Methodist minister "Mr. Prindle," in announcing an upcoming camp meeting, was quoted saying this about the last one: "The Rev. Gentleman mentions that, at their last Camp Meeting, they '*were disturbed by none but Drunkards*,' and he hoped that, as the cause of Temperance had progressed, rapidly, that they should see none of that *species* among them."[6] Both sections of the country faced the same kind of human impediments in securing a righteous gathering in the wilderness and both regions were overly optimistic that the kind of *species* that invariably showed up to thwart spiritual progress might one day cease to be. Thus both sections were equally shocked by what happened to Sarah Maria Cornell at the hands of a Methodist preacher. The *Boston Morning Post* on May 23, 1833, noted it would "commence . . . publication of this highly interesting trial . . . and shall continue it until it is concluded."[7] Down in Huntsville, Alabama, the *Democrat* in that city began publishing a series of granular articles, almost stenographic in appearance and detail, concerning the "Trial of E. K. Avery."[8] The *Democrat* was following other newspapers in picking up the *Boston Morning Post* coverage and publishing it verbatim. Beginning on February 14, 1833, the *Democrat* carried two articles on page 4 related to the murder, one noting that Preacher Avery had "absconded and a reward offered for his apprehension by the State of Rhode Island," and the other where the preacher had been found and arrested in New Hampshire, disguised "by allowing his whiskers to grow, which previously had always been shaved."[9]

In the years after the trial, even into the twentieth century, the death of Sarah Maria Cornell was remembered for the shocking nature of her death and what came to light in the courtroom.

> The trial probably excited greater interest throughout the country than that of almost any similar case on record, from the standing of

the accused as well as the peculiar complications which characterized the case.[10]

> The murder [*sic*] which in some of its aspects surpassed anything in the history of the United States, came to light on the morning of Dec. 21, 1832.[11]

The latter quotation was from 1909, when, more than seventy-five years after her death, Sarah Maria Cornell's remains were moved from one cemetery to another in Fall River, Massachusetts. The move momentarily rekindled the history and sad tale surrounding the factory-worker's death and the twenty-seven-day trial of the Methodist minister charged with killing her. It was but a spark of remembrance in a local setting in 1909, nothing like 1832–33, when the story made its way down to Alabama and shocked a young nation that believed it was possible to Christianize America to the glory of God and betterment of humans and society, and the camp meeting was one way of accomplishing that. Now, in 1833, came testimony such as the following: "a sketch of the testimony of Dr. Wilbur," the Fall River physician who treated Sarah Maria Cornell:

> I hereby certify that a young lady calling herself Sarah M. Cornell, called on me between the fifth and tenth of the tenth month last, and wished me to examine her and decide if possible what her desease [*sic*] might be, if any. On proceeding, as usual in such an investigation, I informed her that I was unable to discover any derangement in the functions of life—and added, that people were generally satisfied if they could get relief after giving their physician all the information *they* possessed. She then says, 'I have been a wicked girl. I have reason to suppose, that I am like to have a child. And wish you to tell me whether such is my case or not.' I then informed her that it was impossible for me to decide unless advanced in pregnancy. She then says, 'if I am in such a condition, it is of but short standing not to exceed about six weeks; for I had never had intercourse with any man until the time of the Methodist camp meeting in Thompson, the present fall, [and] was then invited by a man of high standing to take a walk from the camp ground, and talk over a difference which

> existed between us. After straying some ways from the congregation, he said that the only condition, on which he would settle the difference, was, that he should enjoy sexual intercourse with me, promising at the same time, that if I would consent to it, that he would do me no mischief. It was dark or dusk, I was in his power, and finally consented. He assured me positively, that I should experience no ill from what he had done, and charged me never to disclose the fact. Our settlement was now finished, and we returned to the camp ground.'[12]

On Sarah Cornell's fourth visit to see Dr. Wilbur, one he recalled taking place shortly after the Methodists held a protracted meeting in Fall River, she told the doctor she talked to the Reverend Avery twice during the event. She informed him of her suspicion that their sexual encounter at the Thompson camp meeting had left her with child. He was surprised and, citing his years of experience with his wife, was ready to swear that he did not impregnate her. She assured the preacher if she was pregnant, it could only be his. He told her they would meet again. At the second meeting the minister told Sarah Cornell he had rather give her fifty dollars to get rid of the pregnancy—advising her to purchase "oil of Tansey" to drink. Dr. Wilbur advised her against it, noting it would endanger her life. "She further observed, that Avery said, if she should be likely to have a child, that if she would keep his name from the world, and not swear it, that he would settle with her to her satisfaction hereafter. She was now very anxious that Mr. Avery's name should not be exposed, for she says, he is a very respectable man, has a wife and children, and is a man no one would suspect of being guilty of such an offence. He stands very high among the methodists, and it would be a cause of great disturbance in the methodist church, and it would ruin the man forever, if the fact should get out." At that point, Dr. Wilbur said Sarah Cornell left without asking for any of the medicine he had been treating her with since, presumably, she was convinced by then that "it will do me no good" and that the "disease" was pregnancy.

The "difference" that existed between Sarah Maria Cornell and the Reverend Mr. Avery appeared to go back to Lowell, Massachusetts, where she was a member of his congregation. The testimony of Grindell Rawson, Sarah Cornell's brother-in-law, during the trial of Avery was recorded this way: "Sarah told witness and his wife that at the Thompson camp meeting the following transaction took place between Mr. Avery and her. She said she met him on the ground on Thursday, and he requested her to meet him in the evening at a certain house, when the horn blew for preaching; that they walked from there into a wood; that she asked him if he had burned certain confessional letters she had sent to him; that he replied 'no'; and said 'there is one condition upon which I will burn them, and settle the difficulty'; and that when they parted he had agreed to burn the letters."[13]

Those so-called "confessional letters" would play a huge role in the way the victim was portrayed during the trial of E. K. Avery. Was she insane and capable of suicide or a poor soul victimized by a preacher; was she telling the truth when she told Dr. Thomas Wilbur that she'd never had intercourse with a man prior to the Thompson camp meeting or was she lying? Dr. William Graves from Lowell testified that he saw Sarah Maria Cornell, who gave her name as "Maria S. Connell," on August 30, 1830, and she was "very severely afflicted" with *lues venereal*—venereal disease.[14] Dr. Graves said Sarah Cornell called on him seven times between August 30 and September 20, 1830. He also testified that on one occasion he overheard Sarah Cornell blaming E. K. Avery for turning her out of the Lowell church and, on an occasion in the doctor's office, she said, "If a certain Minister know[s] she had got the disease, he would swear a little; and added I would rather drown myself than that he should know it." Another doctor, Noah Martin from Great Falls, said he gave Sarah Cornell a prescription for medicine for "*chronic gonorrhea*," a condition he said "was apparently of long standing." Dr. Martin also testified that Sarah Cornell told him that Dr. Graves in Lowell "had conducted himself indiscreetly," meaning that her venereal disease had come to the knowledge of Preacher Avery and she had been dismissed from the Methodist church in Lowell as a result. According to Dr. Martin's account, she had caught the "disease" when she came to the attention of a young merchant in Lowell who asked her to ride out on a Sunday afternoon, whereupon the couple presented themselves as man and wife in the place they stayed, slept in the same bed, and that's how she came to be diseased. Also according to Dr. Martin's testimony, Sarah Cornell said Preacher Avery should

have been satisfied with dismissing her from the church in Lowell, but "had made communications respecting her" that was preventing her from joining another church. Other witnesses, such as Nathan Howard of Norwich, Massachusetts, said that, starting in July 1830, rumors were afoot concerning Sarah Cornell's "illicit connexion [*sic*] with different men," that she had confessed to him of a theft charge against her and thereafter "that she had attempted to destroy herself." A part of Howard's testimony appeared this way in the newspaper: "I brought charges against her before the Methodist Episcopal Church at Lowell on the first of October 1830, for fornication and lying, and she was consequently expelled." Nathan Howard further said he next saw Sarah Cornell on the "first Sabbath in June 1831" near the Methodist meetinghouse where she spoke to him and acknowledged the truth of the charges against her. According to what he said, she told him "she had experienced great temptation to destroy herself, which she should do at some future period. . . . An appearance of wildness" is the way Nathan Howard described Sarah Cornell at that chance meeting.

It was either suicide or murder, and the first knee-jerk conclusion was suicide. John Durfee of Tiverton, Rhode Island, a witness at the trial, found the body on his property on the morning of December 21, 1832:

> "A female hanging to a stake . . . hair hanging over her face; parted it to see if she was dead or alive; she had a cloak on, one hook open opposite the breast; calash [hood] on; calash back on right side, the cord in contact with the right cheek, passing forward of the ear; shoes off, feet close together, toes touching the ground, knees bent forward, within 4 or 6 inches of the ground, bent under her knees, and reaching close to the instep; her shoes laying about 18 inches on, right side of her feet, mud on one; handkerchief some distance on left side; gloves on; could not slip the cord up the stake, & cut the cord within half an inch from the stake, and 4 from her neck; procured the Coroner who charged the jury in the stack yard, after which the body was removed to witness' house in a wagon, wrapped in a blanket, and laying on some hay; carried slow; when taken down laid on her side, her bent knees preventing her from being laid otherwise."[15]

In 1909, when Sarah Cornell's remains were moved from one cemetery to another, the events of that December 21, 1832, morning and what followed were recalled from Dr. Thomas Wilbur's perspective: "He followed a curious crowd of women who ran frantically past his door and found the body of a young woman suspended from a stake beside a hay stack on the Durfee farm. Pushing back the hair that had fallen over her face, recognized in the victim, his caller of a previous night."[16] That look back in 1909 concluded that the coroner's jury, apparently authorized on the spot that December morning in 1832, was criticized at the time for its hasty conclusion that the dead woman was a suicide. John Durfee, the property owner, in spite of what was referred to in 1909 as "the peculiar circumstances," decided that Sarah Cornell deserved a decent burial and arranged for her to be buried in his family plot in a private cemetery "on the west side of Forest street." It would appear that it was from that cemetery that Sarah Cornell's remains were removed in 1909. It was noted the women who prepared her body for burial in 1832, "found several pieces of soiled paper beside the body and later where the girl roomed, several letters. The soiled paper bore the message: 'If I am missing enquire of the Rev. E. K. Avery,— Sarah M. Cornell.' In the excitement none of them thought to speak of the find. The funeral was held the next day, and then developments came fast." Indeed, in short order the message Sarah Cornell left behind became known, and one Thomas Hart produced a comb he found "many yards from where the body was discovered." The comb belonged to Sarah Cornell. All of it created a buzz, and the coroner ordered the body exhumed; that's when it was discovered that the "clove hitch" around the dead woman's neck could not have been tightened by the victim but required another person to be present at her death. The gloves she was wearing bore no marks that she herself handled the rope that choked the life from her. Now the coroner's verdict changed to murder. The people of Fall River "had become thoroughly aroused" and voted at a meeting to do everything possible to help Rhode Island authorities find and prosecute the murderer. During that time, the Rev. E. K. Avery had fled Bristol, Connecticut, for New Hampshire, fearing the Fall River mob. That's where the preacher was arrested.

On May 6, 1833, the Methodist preacher was arraigned on a charge of murdering Sarah Maria Cornell: "The indictment contained 3 counts:—The first alleged that the defendant on the 20th fastened a small cord around her neck, and strangled her: the 2$^{d}$ that he tied the cord round her neck, and hung her to a stake: the 3$^{d}$ that he inflicted certain mortal bruises, on her back, side and abdomen; that he then squeezed or compressed her throat, strangled her, and hung her to a stake."[17] After nearly two hundred witnesses testified during the long trial, some of them remembered Sarah Cornell as a "bad girl" with a reputation who showed up on the camp grounds, Preacher E. K. Avery was acquitted of the murder charges against him. Members of the jury deliberated for sixteen hours, and it was said of them that they appeared "with faces haggard, care worn and severe"; that ten of the twelve "found no difficulty in upon coming to a verdict of not guilty," while they were "equally divided" on the suicide question.[18] Concerning the Thompson, Connecticut, camp meeting where the Methodist preacher allegedly had sex with his former congregant and impregnated her, it was recalled in 1909 how ministers and laymen alike came forward at the trial and essentially provided an alibi for E. K. Avery for every minute at the camp meeting.

The New England Conference of the Methodist Episcopal Church no sooner heard about the jury's acquittal than they moved to discredit the dead factory girl and restore the minister to his station. A committee was appointed by the conference to look into Avery's possible expulsion from the church after his acquittal. What the committee reported was that "in the annals of criminal jurisprudence" no nonpolitician had ever incurred more prejudice and perusal than had E. K. Avery; that, in spite of the bias and prejudice and array of testimony against him, he was acquitted, and only truth and innocence could endure such a crucible.[19] What of the sexual relationship between Avery and Sarah Maria Cornell? The committee found no evidence of that intimacy; it claimed she made it up; the preacher had an air-tight alibi at the camp meeting. There was no intimacy, only revenge in Sarah Cornell's heart at being dismissed from the Lowell church. That wasn't to say Sarah Cornell didn't have what the Methodist committee called "her paramour, for one she must have had, there was disgrace and perhaps conjugal infidelity to be covered." The Reverend Avery's deportment, however, was deemed remarkable under the circumstances. The Methodists resolved that their minister was "innocent . . . of any criminal intercourse with Sarah M. Cornell, and of any other act connected with this unhappy affair, at all involving his Christian or ministerial character." Therefore, he was to be returned to ministerial office and church privileges, and it was suggested the Bishop appoint him to a church field where he might recover his health.

It wasn't to be that easy, that simple. The lessons to be learned about the world and human nature in the case of E. K. Avery were left for the world to point out. It was as if the Methodist divines who used the camp meeting to save souls couldn't face the realities of the world against which they were positioned as God's champions. Not one visionary seemed to discern the end game. It was the journalist in Choctaw County, Alabama, who signaled the warning about the slinky, carnal-minded fellow watching the ladies outside the church door or in the camp meeting, while Baptist William Ashcraft could see all kinds of sensuality and carnality in dancing and the ballroom, but never seemed to allow for the same thrills at the camp meeting. Likewise, when the Rev. Isaac S. Kalloch went to trial in 1857 for adultery, it was a case of history repeating the E. K. Avery trial. This trial also featured the detail the so-called "public press" went into in covering the evidence; the public opinion pressing in on the legal proceeding; and the circus atmosphere around a clergyman involved in illicit sex.[20] The jury couldn't agree—eight were for acquittal, four for conviction—so the preacher was acquitted. Again, it was the press, not the ministers, able to see clearly where the pilgrimage for the Reverend Kalloch was headed: "Often times, though the decision of a court may declare the accused innocent, it does not avail nor save him from ruin. E. K. Avery was acquitted by the jury; but he was as much dead from the hour of his arrest, as though he had ceased to breathe; nor has he been able to hold his head up in society since. . . . It must end so, we think, with Mr. Kalloch. His people will support him for a time, as the Methodists did Avery; but his usefulness has ended." Indeed, E. K. Avery's name and example would be invoked before and after the incident regarding his fellow minister Kalloch. By early September 1833, just months after his trial ended, it was reported that Avery was retiring from public office, "until the public shall become fully satisfied of his innocence . . . that God in his providence will ere long remove every possible doubt from the minds of all in relation to his painful and mysterious case."[21] That was difficult when writings related to the sensational trial were still appearing. In early 1833, Col. Harvey Harnden seems to have written a pamphlet about his arrest of E. K. Avery in New Hampshire, a first-person account that perhaps presented the author in heroic terms.[22] Then, too, the Methodists said a pamphlet of their own was forthcoming, one that would not only vindicate the result of the trial but present "a mass of evidence" that was excluded in court.[23] Any and everything could be a reminder of the shame that was supposed to have started at the Thompson camp meeting. When they tore down the "Old South" building in Fall River in 1835—"that old dilapidated barrack, the receptacle of man and beast, drunk and sober, whose pulpit has been defiled with scenes that would have put to the blush the inhabitants of Sodom and Gomorrah"—it was the place "where was held the last interview between the vile E. K. Avery and his fair victim S. M. Cornell, before the final clove hitch was embedded in her neck."[24] Even after twenty years of quiet, uneventful farming, he was still the preacher who was once tried for murder.[25] He was referred to as "Rev. 'Rhode Island' Avery" in 1868 when his son, Frank, was killed on the railroad, only the people of Richmond, Massachusetts, where Avery spent his early years, didn't want to acknowledge the connection.[26] Let's just move on, they said. Even in 1919 a ninety-year-old woman could recall Preacher Avery being "hung in effigy on the old buttonwood tree which stood near her home, and that the effigy was made in the barn of her great-grandfather, Col. Durfee," Durfee land being where the body of Sarah Cornell was discovered.[27] When a big-city newspaper article in 1930 looked back a hundred years and noted a "notorious" person named "Mr. E. K. Avery," it wondered if he was a "counterpart" of a fellow named Capone "or other allegedly notorious men of today."[28] The 1930 newspaper couldn't tell from the story it printed from "The Sun" in 1833. It seemed this Avery fellow caused excitement on a Hartford steamboat when passengers became aware that he was onboard. They complained to the captain, and the captain said that had he known who the man was before the boat left the wharf, he would have declined him as a passenger. When the boat stopped at Middletown, a crowd had assembled and Mr. Avery had to "force his way to the Methodist parsonage in that place." The fact that six hundred thousand Methodists held E. K. Avery in full fellowship was deemed "conniving at iniquity" by one person, who was likely not alone in that opinion.[29]

God wasn't renowned for His sense of humor in those days, but the shock and tragic circumstances that came out of the murder trial of E. K. Avery offered proof that human nature simply can't resist tempting the Almighty's patience. One government entity entertained legislation that would have made E. K. Avery chaplain at the "Ohio Penitentiary," cited as perhaps the only means available of putting the man in prison.[30] The following witticism appeared in a couple of Alabama newspapers.[31] It seems Jeremy Mason, an eminent New England lawyer, was on E. K. Avery's defense team and having trouble coming up with evidence to defend the preacher. A well-known clergyman rushed in one day and said with excitement that he had "evidence that will clear brother [*sic*] Avery." It seems in a dream the angel Gabriel appeared to the clergyman and announced that Avery was innocent. Replied Mason, "Very good, sir; then take that summons and have it served on Gabriel at once." Yet another Alabama newspaper told the story of how P. T. Barnum, the circus showman, was taught a lesson involving the Rev. Ephraim K. Avery.[32] In 1836, early in Barnum's show business career, he joined Aaron Turner's circus as ticket seller and held various other positions. In Annapolis, Maryland, as the show was making ready to perform,

> Barnum in a new suit of black broadcloth started for a walk, when Turner called the attention of bystanders to him, saying that he was the Rev. E. K. Avery, who had recently been acquitted of the murder of a young woman, and against whom there was a deep feeling of aversion. Barnum was immediately followed. The crowd soon became a mob, a rail was produced, and the throng were about to ride him on it, when Barnum succeeded in convincing them that he was not the clergyman, but a showman connected with the circus. With his new coat hanging in tatters he went to Turner and indignantly asked the meaning of the practical joke.

"My dear Barnum," said the old man, "it was all for our good. Remember, all we need to insure success is notoriety."[33]

The Avery mess wouldn't die. He was, if not a man for all seasons, a man for all reasons. Want to draw a big crowd under the big top? Use Preacher Avery's notoriety. If you're proslavery and hate abolitionists, make "the R. Island murderer" an abolitionist.[34] A rumor that he'd died (he hadn't!)? An opportunity to beat a dead horse and say in print, in spite of the improbability, that on his deathbed he confessed to killing not only Sarah Maria Cornell, but also two other women.[35] Or, at his rumored death, make him a teamster, carpenter, and occasional preacher who drew the whole population when he preached.[36] Add to Avery's detractors those who wanted to believe in the preacher's innocence and never ceased trying to exonerate him. One story was that a man and boy who could have provided the preacher with an air-tight alibi the night Sarah Cornell was killed—they were herding sheep but were never found at the time the trial occurred—had been found in Bristol, England, and corroborated Avery's side of the story.[37] Another story was that a sea captain said years after the killing that a passenger on his vessel in route to Bangor, Maine, told him he knew E. K. Avery was innocent of the killing since the whole matter was set up by the unnamed passenger.[38] The passenger was enraged because Avery had expelled him from the Lowell church, and he plotted revenge this way.

> The man said that being about Avery's size and appearance, he procured a hat and cloak resembling closely those that Avery usually wore, white neckcloth included, and persistently watched for a long time his opportunity to appear in her company (at *evening* always) to lead people to believe that it was Avery that was in her society. Further, he said that . . . at the very hour of the evening service at Thompson, Conn., he was with Miss Cornell in the woods adjacent to the camp ground.
>
> This man further stated . . . that he knew Miss Cornell's intention to commit suicide, for she had threatened it to him; and as soon as he learned of her death, he went out West and remained some time before he returned East.

The Thompson, Connecticut, camp meeting was an aberration when compared to most camp meetings of the nineteenth century; it was a singular example of the brutality, conspiracies, cover-ups and worst inclinations of humanity that could result in that setting. That history hyperbolized that one camp meeting is true, but that exaggerated example perhaps helped form the basis of those tepid warnings issued later in camp meetings in Alabama—namely, watch out for that leering, poison-tongued guy and heed those benign-sounding references regarding courtships, matrimonial alliances, and young couples pairing off. Things went on in tents and under the oaks—"imprudent" things! The less said of it the better.

If sin is missing the mark, well, Alabamans didn't completely miss the target with sex at the camp meeting. They knew; they just didn't want to know too much. No doubt, when the story of the Rev. Ephraim K. Avery made its way to Dixie those who read it must have shaken their heads at the awfulness of it; they must have wondered if such wickedness was a sign of the end times. Yet, in 1833, when the Methodists rushed to welcome back E. K. Avery into the fold following his acquittal, they offered in his defense this explanation of how a man of character and moral standing could have faced such prejudice and heavy-handed prosecution: "Where every mind was on alert, and every eye and ear was open, every man, woman, and child, that had any possible knowledge of a possible circumstance, would be drawn forth. Under such an influence, also, strengthened and magnified as everything must be by mutual excitement, shadows become embodied into substantial forms, dreams are changed into realities, and vague impressions become known and vivid conceptions."[39] Without knowing it, the Methodists, as it were, explained the psychology of the camp meeting they championed perhaps more than any other religious group. People, as one, were swept up in a spirit—not necessarily *the Spirit*. This created a domino effect in which, fueled by group excitement, shadows take on substance, dreams become the real thing, imagination becomes fact, leading to "what was at first stated cautiously, and as mere conjecture, [becoming] in the lapse of time, *positive* testimony."

The second name in the alphabetized list of felons in *Crimes of Preachers*, referenced at the beginning of this chapter, had no date for his crimes. His residence was listed as "Tiverton, R.I.[,] Fall River, Mass.[,] Bristol, R.I. [and] Ohio." He was a Methodist and under "Crime Charged" this: "Seduction, adultery, and murder; married." The "Preacher's Name" appeared as "Avery, Rev. Eph. K." Perhaps the reason there was no date was that his crime seemed somehow outside the pale of belief and possibility, as if he was something born of nightmare, a devil posing as a divine, almost an archetypal warning to beware of such a poseur.

If the camp meeting was about impressions, well, it was possible to be mistaken about both the institution of religious camping and what it was intended to promote. It's like the little newspaper notice of fifty words or so that appeared in 1885 that referenced a bill passed in the Alabama House of Representatives that would prohibit camp meetings in certain parts of Geneva County.[40] Only, what the newspaper had meant to say was that "camp hunting" was prohibited. The error must have caused a stir based on the correction: "So the people of Geneva county are not interfered with in their right to meet and praise God under the green trees. Awkward mistakes will happen sometimes." One word mistakenly substituted for another, even when it completely changes the meaning, is understandable; it's human; it's a slip-up; there's no long-term damage. But when mistakes are never corrected and go unchecked they become history. It's like the story of the fourteen-year-old boy, described as being of an "exceptionally nervous temperament," who got saved at camp meeting.[41] He insisted on becoming a preacher. His youth and evangelistic fire drew crowds wherever the "Boy Evangelist" appeared and "feverish excitement" followed. Yet, he was still just a child, and his sermons had no substance, "only wild, incoherent cries, which excited his own emotional nature to the uttermost." Over time his hearers recognized the emptiness in his words, so he resorted to showmanship, such as running up and down the aisles as he preached and standing on one leg. He became a spiritual clown, his "mind . . . impaired; the long nervous strain had unseated his reason." Alabama campers separated themselves from the world at set times and seasons, sought God in the wilderness at brush arbors, and knelt in the pine straw, and still missed the message. Whether the show and showmanship drowned out the full message or the message was only feverish excitement to begin with isn't the point as much as something that was said about the clownish boy evangelist: he tried to become a teacher before he became a learner.

It probably isn't fair to invoke the Reverend Fendley right here, but perhaps he wouldn't mind if it's for the purpose of history, although he'd probably be more comfortable with "spiritual instruction" as the reason for doing so. Whatever, he's called upon regarding the lack of discernment that sometimes accompanied Alabama campers to the wilderness or gripped them while at camp, as if the frenzy and fresh air could quell that gift of the spirit. The reverend is a cautionary tale in the sense that, if a solid Christian soldier like him could lack discernment, and that could lead to a tragic circumstance, well, everybody best take note.

Take it from me, you can feel the temptation when you're standing at a railroad crossing blocked by a train that hasn't moved for what seems like an eternity. Baking in the hot sun with dust clouds from the log yard swirling around you, or freezing and shivering in winter, or just being a kid and wanting to get on with the next important activity, it's the Devil, your id, or some ill-defined goading that wells up and tells you to just climb over the coupling between the cars, or just dart under a boxcar and crab-crawl out the other side before those steel wheels come to life with a lurch up and down the line. It's likely a kind of death-wish contemplation, even if you don't know such a thing exists as a kid. But surely a fifty-nine-year-old preacher, steeped in Bible learning and Bible wisdom, would know that it isn't a good idea to crawl under a train. Wouldn't that be a good example of *discernment*, knowing *not* to crawl under a train? But that's exactly what the reverend and his wife, Harriet, did on a day in 1895. It's just one more instance where the reverend and I crossed paths and experiences many years apart; both of us waiting on a train to move, only he in a sawmill town named "Behrman" that would be renamed "Fulton" by the time I came along. One difference is I never played Russian roulette with a train. Locally, what happened was reported this way: "The wife of Rev. J. H. Fendley, while attempting to pass under and between two cars of a freight at Behrman, last Saturday, had an arm broken in two places."[42] A week later, under a headline that included the words "Unnecessary

Risk," for that it most certainly was, the news was worse: "Sunday night as a Mobile & Birmingham freight train was standing at Burman [*sic*] station, seventy miles south of Selma, Rev. and Mrs. J. H. Fendley attempted to crawl under at a road crossing. Mr. Fendley passed under safely, but his wife was run over and her right arm crushed so badly that amputation was necessary."[43]

It's another thing the reverend and I share besides a corner of the living room. We are the embodiments of the frailties and inconsistencies that made the camp meeting in Alabama as unpredictable and fraught with uneasiness as it was supposed to be uplifting and transformative for those who camped. Lest this hero of my family leave behind a less than sterling impression upon the reader due to his descendant's voice and choice of materials, I leave you with what I consider a heroic moment for the man, one that leads this writer to the conviction that the best we can hope for in ourselves and others is precisely that—a moment or two along the way when we step up and perform some small courageous act that's worth remembering. That's enough in a world that is, sadly, ever ready to take even sacred moments and use them in vile displays of evil doing. An example of that follows.

# 5

## "And I Remember the Names and Characters of the Men Who Engaged in It"

As noted, the reverend's ministry from the sources wasn't about the grandeur of angels ascending and descending "Jacob's Ladder," or Isaiah's vision of the Lord high and lifted up. It was about matters typically related to everyday uneventful and prosaic ministry; the stuff that barely qualified as "spiritual," and, no doubt, the reverend must at times have felt that "plowing" the fields "white unto harvest" in hopes of a bounty of souls for Jesus wasn't all that different from the monotony of plowing the hard, packed earth he had forsaken in order to preach, with just as many impediments to turning up a straight furrow. Also, there's no evidence that the reverend was faced with any of the larger issues roiling Baptist life in the South during those days, such as Landmarkism. That was a movement propelled by the belief that the origins of the Baptist church went back to the time of Jesus and John the Baptist, a theory advanced before the Civil War by J. R. Graves, a Tennessee editor. The Southern Baptist Convention tried to separate itself from Landmark influences, but some of J. R. Graves's ideas—the most prominent being that there was a line of succession traced through a "trail of blood" back to Jesus, and the hesitancy to recognize ministers, churches, and Christians that couldn't trace their origins the same way—were hard to eradicate. In 1893, Prof. William Heth Whitsitt of Southern Baptist Theological Seminary in Louisville, Kentucky, wrote an article in which he said the practice of baptism by immersion for Baptists didn't start until the seventeenth century in

England. Landmarkism's "trail of blood" back to apostolic times was predicated on baptism by immersion being traceable back to John the Baptizer, so Whitsitt stirred up a regional hornets' nest with his scholarship. Landmark influence was such among Southern Baptists that, by 1899, Whitsitt, by then president of the seminary, was forced to resign. Still, there exists no specific evidence that matters of baptism and ecclesiology were issues the reverend was directly confronted with, though it's highly likely that Landmark ideology was held by some Baptists in his circle of preachers and church members. Certainly, lack of both controversy and in-church fighting isn't to imply that the reverend's ministry was routine to the point of being dull and boring. After all, you never knew when a murder might pop up.

On a Saturday night in December 1888, near Lower Peach Tree in Wilcox County, a white man named Sam Walker was killed by a shotgun blast. The killing was the result of what was referred to as a "difficulty" Walker had with a Black man named Fred (his name sometimes appearing as "Fed") Kidd on two previous occasions.[1] The shooting occurred as Walker and a friend were returning home. The friend was wounded in the arm, but Walker was "killed instantly, leaving a wife and one child." Fred Kidd and other Blacks were arrested and jailed. Fred Kidd was eventually sentenced to death by hanging for the murder. A year later, Kidd, awaiting the gallows in January 1890, still refused to confess and had but one request, namely, a Christmas dinner, which, it was reported, his lawyer "promised cheerfully."[2] When the time came, Fred Kidd's hanging was reported this way. Fred, for some time anxious to get on with things, had been impatient for death's arrival.[3] He walked with steady step from his jail cell to the gallows and climbed the steps to the platform the same way. Once the hood was put over his head and the rope adjusted, however, Fred Kidd broke down and was unable to stand. According to the newspaper account, it was as if the man realized he was standing at the threshold of "death and eternity." Because he was overwhelmed and unable to stand, the rope stayed taut and, as a result, when he dropped the fall wasn't sufficient to break his neck. He choked to death, although the local reporting noted he didn't struggle much and died in less time than might have been supposed under the circumstances. Up in Montgomery the reporting said Fred

Kidd's knees trembled, he fell back, was caught and held up, and "the door knocked from under him."[4]

In 1920, thirty years after Fred Kidd's hanging, the county seat weekly in Grove Hill revisited the circuit court session from 1889 regarding the murder trial.[5] In the look back, the judge—"Judge Clarke"—appeared as a kind of surrogate evangelist, appealing to the condemned man this way: "It now only remains for you to prepare to meet your Maker. God has promised to forgive sins, and He will forgive you if you repent and ask him aright, having faith in the Christian religion." But on the grim day of the actual hanging, as the realization of the moment seized Fred Kidd and overwhelmed him, there was a real preacher on hand, one who climbed the gallows with the condemned man and prayed for him. That preacher cited in the accounts was the Rev. J. H. Fendley.

Once, when I was a kid, my great grandmother, Leona Beagle, who was married to one of the reverend's sons, John Joseph Fendley, when he died young in 1898, told me she saw a horse thief hanged when she was a girl. I never thought to ask her what it was like to witness such a shocking event. There were so many hangings back in those days, and so many of them were *botched* hangings of Blacks and whites alike; some of them a lot worse than Fred Kidd's. The reverend, however, was no stranger to shock and horror. He had seen it on a massive scale during the Civil War, for instance in 1863 as he looked out over the wounded and dead near Ringgold, Georgia. The hanging of Fred Kidd was bad enough based on the description, but it was nothing like a hanging that occurred in neighboring Choctaw County nearly eight years earlier. At that Choctaw hanging, there was no Christian leaven present in the person of a man like the Reverend Fendley, a man described by one historian years before the Choctaw hanging took place as "one of the truly live, earnest, original, growing pastors of Bethel Association."[6] No, the Choctaw hanging was the result of allegations about the horrors in store at one of the most sacred institutions of the day. It was about what was allegedly going to happen when godly white men, women, and children, made most vulnerable while under the sweet slaying of the Holy Spirit, would become victims of the national nightmare that had always plagued the American Dream. The sacred institution was the camp meeting. The nightmare scenario was Black revolt or revenge. What happened in 1882 is best understood in the context of what was going on back then and even earlier.

Simply stated, there were two types of religious camp meetings in Alabama: one for whites, one for Blacks. The white camp meeting was a serious matter in spite of the ruffians and rowdies that invariably turned up like bad pennies. The Black camp meeting was essentially no different as regarded the sincerity of believers and the turnout of a bad element. Did Black campers ever chuckle at or poke fun of the whims and fancies of white campers seeking the Lord? Probably, though public acknowledgment of that wouldn't have been prudent in the nineteenth century. What is a certainty is that whites found a source of unabashed amusement, derision, and lightheartedness in the Black camping experience wherever it took place. Take the reenactment of the Parable of the Prodigal Son at a Black camp meeting in Hillsborough, Illinois, in 1887. An article concerning the northern camp meeting was reprinted in Montgomery from the *Memphis Avalanche* in Tennessee. In the former, the story was titled "Fatted Calf" with a subhead noting that the calf was killed the day before the "Negro Prodigal" returned, while the latter's headline was "A Colored Prodigal Son."[7] "Elder Jackson, seventy years old, with a great shock of snow-white wool on his head, is the leading and controlling spirit, and to him is due the conception and carrying out of the affair in which the great camp meeting culminated. This was the enactment yesterday and to-day of scenes illustrating the biblical parable of the prodigal son." It's hard not to read the newspapers' account without seeing the entertainment value it had for a white readership in that day. The fatted calf, about two months old, was led to a spot where a "portly butcher" was sharpening a huge knife; the calf trembling while the "colored members of the meeting congregated on the grand stand and consoled [it] by singing 'Fear Not, Trembling One It Is I'"; the calf was disposed of by the butcher's knife, its blood streaming out onto the sacrificial altar, and, as the "last death throes of the animal ceased the chief started up the tune 'I Will Walk Through the Gates of the City,'" whereupon the portly butcher decapitated the calf and got it ready for use the following day. The following day; that's when the prodigal returned, "witnessed by an immense throng of people, white and black. . . . A few minutes before 3 o'clock a blast on the old plantation dinner horn warned the assembled multitude that something was about to happen. As the echoes died away the procession of soldiers marched upon the raised platform. After the singing of several hymns Elder Jackson arose and delivered a sermon on the prodigal son. At the conclusion of the sermon several of the elders made mysterious motions with their hands, as if beckoning to some one [*sic*]; but the prodigal son, concealed behind some shrubbery in some distant field, had forgotten his cue, and it was not until the white-haired Elder Jackson seized the dinner horn and blew a loud, long blast that the ebony-hued prodigal realized that it was time for him to appear." The prodigal, "a ragged red coat and his garments . . . literally in tatters," embraced the "feeble old father" who rushed down off the platform to embrace him in a reunion that was described as "emotional." There was shouting and singing and two thousand people ate the "fatted calf," which was served up with "great chunks of bread." An Illinois newspaper prior to the camp meeting speculated that the meeting at Farmer City might reenact the killing of the fatted calf, but "possums and persimmons" was more like it.[8] A newspaper after the fact said the fatted calf was "barbecued crisp and brown."[9] All of it was fodder for entertainment, perhaps at a white church social or material for a minstrel show, North or South.

Insightful readers of the Selma paper in 1884 might have noted similarities between the races' camping experiences rather than differences. Much discussion regarding camp meetings ensued when the "African M.E. Conference" met in Baltimore, Maryland, in May.[10] Regarding the general conference's position on camp meetings, many speeches were given but few presented the camp meeting in a positive light. The Rev. S. J. Coppin, noting the Christian brothers at the conference wouldn't like, in the newspaper's words, to hear him "speak of the various immoralities that were practiced at camp meetings," made a point that was valid for both Blacks and whites; namely, it was tough enough to control people in regular life, but impossible when they were turned loose in the woods. Likewise, a lot of the people converted in the woods never got around to going to church afterwards. There was a financial component at play, too. Too much expense involved in camp meetings! The Reverend Coppin said that the year before, in one twenty-four-hour period, "the colored people of Baltimore had paid $4,200 to the Railroad Co., in this connection and that, too, when some of the colored people were asking charity." Some preachers at the conference split the difference on the subject. One said they might have immoral camp meetings in Maryland, but they didn't have them in Georgia, where he was from; another Georgian said he wouldn't comment on camp meetings where people got drunk, but he argued that what was termed the "regular old fashioned camp meetings" still had a future. Yet a third preacher from Georgia said he knew of fellow ministers who made a $1,000 each day at camp meetings; whether he considered that a good thing or bad wasn't made clear by the reporting. But there was no mistaking one preacher's position that the day of the camp meeting should be over: "Rev. J. S. Lee, of South Carolina, said camp meetings were held near Spartanburg in that State and that there were six wagon loads of whisky on the grounds during the entire time of meeting. Ministers and elders were under the influence of liquors all the time. He was assaulted with a club by a young man who was murdered at one of these camp meetings."[11]

Actually, loss of life among Blacks was treated with nonchalance, even humor, by whites. Huge crowds of "colored citizens"—three to five thousand of them—headed to Chunnenuggee Ridge in Bullock County in 1889 for a camp meeting, a turnout so large that the Mobile & Eufaula and Mobile & Girard excursion trains "were packed with sweating and sweltering humanity."[12] Many who had bought a ticket couldn't find room on the train and walked. Besides the loss of limb that occurred at the depot regarding the previously mentioned nineteen-year-old Black male, it was reported the train killed two more between the ridge where the camp meeting was held and "Columbus," presumably the city in Georgia. The assessment of the deaths was opined this way: "The wonder is that the disasters were not more numerous and severe. The colored brother will have his fun—a principal item of which is riding to the camp-meeting on 'de kyars,' and he must take the attendant risks." In a separate posting in the same issue it was noted that a train out of Troy filled with colored pilgrims headed for the ridge camp meeting made for an unpleasant trip for the "white travellers" [*sic*], for, "There are some things pleasanter than the odor d'Afrique."

Church squabbles, an all-too-frequent occurrence that called for seasons of prayer and soul searching by white congregations, was viewed in a different light by whites when it was Black church schism. If anything, a church split was both uglier and stereotyped from the white viewpoint when Black religion was involved. "The colored-Baptist-church squabble, having passed, with all its pleasing accompaniments of thick skulls, kinky hair and *odors d'Afrique*, from the holy pale of religion into the idle gossip of town, has now invaded the sacred precincts of the terror-armed and mighty law. Last Saturday, three cullud gemmen were hauled up before Mayor Harrell, charged with disturbing the peace and infringing on the rights of others in that they did on Thursday night last gone open the doors of the church on 'Baptist hill' and attempt to worship god therein."[13] The three Blacks—described as "church-breaking psalm-singers"—were in a trial that lasted from 9 a.m. to 2 p.m. that involved two town lawyers and leading white Baptists called as experts on church polity. Each of the defendants ended up being charged a dollar and court costs. A few months before that, it was the same mayor presiding over what was described as "a flock of soiled doves caught in the classic precincts of that delectable suburb known to fame as Freedmantown."[14] The poison pen of the newspaper said it was a "charge of disorderly conduct at a grand dress ball . . . at one of the palatial residences of that quarter of the city." The best the press could do as far as objectivity was call it a "big meetin'" when the Blacks changed a meeting location from Baptist Hill to Freedmantown,[15] or point out that the barbecue was good, "well cooked and well served," when a large crowd gathered on Baptist Hill, only there was "some very fine shooting" as well, the particulars of which the newspaper didn't know.[16]

Everything about the Black church experience, including the camp meeting, was exaggerated and a curiosity for whites. The Black funeral was portrayed in the white press as a source of entertainment more so than an occasion for grief. The story was told of poor John Rogers, "a colored fellow," who put up fifty dollars to secure four coaches on a train for an excursion to Montgomery.[17] When the train pulled out, however, he had only four passengers. Unfortunately, "there was [*sic*] a number of colored funerals on that day, which proved a greater attraction for the blacks than an excursion." Such was the white perspective, as was a story told by a white woman to a newspaper columnist of the same gender and race.[18] The woman's "colored maid" had recently attended a big colored funeral. When the white "mistress" asked the maid who did the preaching, the maid said she didn't know; that she couldn't get close enough to hear the preacher's name when it was announced. "But you ought to have seen the people who had to be carried out fainting. I certainly did enjoy it!" Another thing: there were too many references to cite in Alabama newspapers regarding small news pieces on Black funeral processions, typically described as "large." The Black preacher, if not portrayed as an outright scoundrel like the aforementioned Rufus Doyle, was shifty and up to no good. "We hear that Prof. J. Taylor and his Panitheopticonicon are still rambling around in Choctaw, and that an exhibition given at 'David's Gospel,' a negro church below Mt. Sterling, broke up in a row, which was somewhat rough on the 'Perfesser.'"[19] The Panitheopticonicon was an early version of the slide projector that seems to have been used in religious dramatizations, but a newspaper at the other end of the state portrayed the man and contrivance this way: "In Choctaw county a negro calling himself Prof. J. Taylor, is beating his fellows out of all their small money with a magic lantern."[20] The Black clergyman was often a comic character, like old snow-white, wool-haired Elder Jackson, directing the Prodigal Son drama with its missed cues and succulent calf. The Black preacher was a stock character at minstrel shows, or "black-cork comedy," as one Alabama newspaper put it.[21]

But, as the poor fatted calf discovered in the production of the Prodigal Son, there was death and destruction possible at camp meetings be they Black or white. Two twentieth-century killings offered evidence that religious camping was not always a "strait gate" leading to salvation as the Sermon on the Mount put it, but a "broad . . . way" that could lead to destruction.

In 1937, it seems a murderous note was passed between two white men at a camp meeting—"a Holy Roller camp meeting near Blue Springs"—that ultimately led to the stabbing death of an elderly

Missionary Baptist preacher in Barbour County in southeastern Alabama.[22] The Rev. Ed Brown's badly decomposed body had been stabbed twenty-six times when it was found under a pile of clothes and quilts in his house. Accounts of the murder at the time had different spellings for the name of one of the suspects, but "Geener Lee Teal," twenty-eight, was described as a man of "eccentric behavior," "mentally deficient," and "definitely sub-normal but not insane."[23] At the holiness camp meeting Teal got a note from Henry Clark, twenty-three, essentially telling him "to come on," and the two men got together later and clubbed the seventy-year-old preacher and farmer in his home with a stick, took his money, and stabbed him.[24] The killing seemed to be motivated by forty acres of land the old preacher owned that would go to Brown's adopted daughter upon his death.[25] She was married to Teal, and one female witness testified that Teal told her they had put poison in the preacher's coffee pot but it didn't kill him. Teal ended up getting life in prison, as did Clark the following year.

It's one thing to get a note at camp meeting that leads to murder, but it's quite another to kill your father at camp meeting. That's what Sharman Stevens, a Black man, was accused of doing in 1903. His case offers a better understanding of how the camp meeting was less about heaven coming to earth for a week or so than just another design on the cultural, social, and political patchwork quilt of Alabama. The facts regarding the "Notorious Parricide," as one newspaper put it,[26] are few as regards the theme of these pages with the exception of this: "having been convicted at the last term of the circuit court of killing his father at a negro camp meeting."[27] The context within which the camp-meeting killing ultimately played out went something like this.

First, before Sharman Stevens became the "second legal hanging" in Randolph County in the eastern part of the state, there was the first legal hanging. That, too, was a Black man, who was named Tom Barsh. He was charged in the December 1902 shooting death of a Black boy, Willie Birdsong, who was in bed when Barsh and two other Blacks broke into the Birdsong house and shot the place up.[28] Barsh was sentenced to hang; the other two men were sent to the penitentiary for life. The sentence against Tom Barsh was carried out on April 10, 1903, in Wedowee, where it was reported the gallows on which the man died was covered up and left standing as "a ghastly warning to other evil-doers."[29] Almost immediately, however, a racial fear, perhaps a deep-seated superstition, that long existed in Alabama came into play; one that imbued the Black Man with almost supernatural abilities and resulted in Black culprits often being described physically as "large," much like the numbers attached to Black funeral processions that crawled through this tiny town or that. In this case, however, it was the rumor that Tom Barsh, left hanging for thirty-two minutes and pronounced dead by six physicians when he was finally taken down from the gallows, had survived hanging.[30] A "silly, . . . criminal lie" it was called, and there was no truth to the rumor that the Randolph County sheriff and his assistants were overly excited and botched the hanging. Yet, the story of Tom Barsh, still alive after being hung, "has reached Richmond, Indianapolis and other out-of-the-way places, and is getting itself properly exploited. We assure our contemporaries that they need have no apprehension of a visit from a resurrected negro. At last accounts Tom was still dead."[31]

From all indications, after killing his father at the camp meeting in late 1902, Sharman Stevens fled, was on the run for a couple of months, and, during that time, was implicated as the "guilty wretch" in an assault upon a white woman.[32] When he was captured, a mob was organized to lynch him, so he was brought on a train to Opelika for safekeeping. Threats were made to the effect that, if the death penalty didn't result from the charge of killing his father, well, Sharman Stevens would be lynched anyway. After mere minutes of deliberation, the jury returned with the death-penalty sentence, and the big crowd in the courtroom clapped.

Between the hanging of Tom Barsh and the impending hanging of Sharman Stevens, a simmering newspaper war flamed up. On one side was the *Roanoke Leader*, which accused Randolph County Sheriff A. J. Kent of conducting the hanging of Tom Barsh in too public a manner.[33] The hanging resulted, in the newspaper's opinion, in a large crowd assembling in Wedowee that "included some of the hardest characters in the county, as well as many respectable men and even ladies." The upshot was what the *Leader* called "public disorder and demoralization, such as drinking and fighting, extending for miles out on the highways in various directions." In the *Leader*'s words, criticizing the sheriff brought forth "a spiteful spiel from the Randolph Star, the sheriff's personal organ, calculated to wither to the ground any man who dared to exercise his perogative [*sic*] as a free citizen in criticizing the infallible sheriff." The *Leader* was hoping the upcoming September execution of Sharman Stevens would be conducted more privately as the law demanded, thus sparing the county the circus of bad behavior that had accompanied the Barsh hanging. The editor of the *Leader* buttressed his viewpoint by citing the state criminal code and the opinions of Alabama Attorney General Massey Wilson, Circuit Judge N. D. Denson, and Probate Judge Stell Blake, all seemingly supporting the *Leader*'s call for a more private, less sensational execution.

The following week in the *Leader*'s pages a kind of call-and-response appeared in which the *Randolph Star* ("Wedowee Star") countered the hanging issue as the *Leader* stated it in its September 9, 1903, issue, and the *Leader* responded point by point to the *Star*.[34] That issue also carried a long defense by Sheriff Kent, who cited his own authorities for sanctioning the Barsh hanging carried out the way it was, and a response to a *Star* assertion that the *Leader* was jealous that the upcoming hanging of Sharman Stevens might result in the Wedowee dispensary selling "goods" that might otherwise be sold in the Roanoke dispensary.[35] (Dispensaries were government-run liquor dispensers meant to be an anti-saloon measure that would cut down on the public's consumption of alcohol.) Two days before Sharman Stevens was hanged the *Leader* gave up the editorial fight. It was clear Sheriff Kent wasn't going to reform his execution methods.[36] There would be no enclosure to separate the man that would dangle at the end of a rope from the crowd that came to gawk at him swinging. A state newspaper outside the *Leader* vs. *Star* feud recorded the day of the Stevens's hanging in Wedowee this way: "From private correspondence it is learned there was $345.85 worth of whisky sold at the dispensary there on that day. Five thousand people were present, four counties being represented. Old, tottering men and women attended. Every form of conveyance was used by which the people could get there. People were coming in all the night before and continued to roll in up to the hour of the hanging."[37]

In the two murders above the camp meeting was a place and event in a string of places and events that constituted larger dramas; a momentary backdrop—a point in time, just part of the scenery in two cases of tragedy, one white, one Black. Yet, that's the way it had always been with religious camping. Camping was a bit-player in the state drama that invariably showcased the same stock characters, much like the minstrel shows, only these were the mob threatening violence and lynching; the unyielding, heavy-handed sheriff; politicians and newspapers opining on such matters as spirits while the human spirit went neglected; the misguided, finding entertainment in the shadow cast by the gallows. The camp meeting largely reflected the world it claimed to flee like some great speckled bird. Religion was always playing second fiddle to the cast of worldly Alabama characters, making the lone, solitary victim the lesson that might be learned from history. Over half a century before two guys colluded to kill a Primitive Baptist preacher at Blue Springs, something occurred in Alabama that might have served as a template for future understanding but didn't. If the case of the Rev. Ephraim K. Avery in New England had shock value regarding clergy and sex, shock that might have served as an "awakening," the same can be said of Choctaw County, Alabama, in 1882, regarding race. Sadly, once again, no awakening resulted. Regarding the latter, let's put it this way.

Say you got your crops in on time or, if you had a business, say you got your business affairs in order by camp-meeting time.

Say you were self-sustaining and had your wood, cook stove, and provisions set.

Say your tent, be it canvas or boards, was ready for camping.

Say your wagon and horses were ready for a trip to the woods or wilderness.

Say, if you were a young lady, you had your umbrella and dime novel packed.[38]

Say the weather was good—no downpours or drought-stoked dust clouds.

Say there was no outbreak of illness, such as *cholera morbus*.[39]

Say the preaching lineup included luminaries well known for bringing the Holy Spirit down on saints and sinners alike.

Say things looked good as far as law and order on the campground.

Say the dalliances between the young men and young women were nothing more than adolescent crushes that, God willing, might one day lead from the brush arbor to the church altar and marriage.

Say everything was as perfect as could be when, suddenly, darkness descends and your worst nightmare becomes reality. It isn't a wolf howling or a war whoop rising or horse thieves scuttling around the camp meeting. It isn't some Book of Revelation exegesis, three points and a poem, thundered by some wizened preacher stabbing at the night air with his bony finger. No, it's *the* Great Fear, namely, a race war; Blacks plotting rebellion and insurrection and viciously falling upon innocent white campers seeking the Lord Almighty. That had been white America's collective bad dream since the country was founded and now, from the looks of it, two of the Four Horsemen of the Apocalypse—War and Death—had galloped straight into Choctaw County in the middle of camp-meeting season. There was this Black general, his army, his secret, murderous plans, and, had it not been for a fluke, well. . . .

The fluke was that a white boy, said to have been twelve to fourteen years of age, found a "bundle of papers" in the roadway not far from his home in Desotoville on Tuesday morning, August 15, 1882, "Desotoville precinct . . . at a point almost 12 miles northwest of Butler and a mile and a half or two miles south of the Camp Ground, a place mentioned several times in the papers, and which has been used every fall for several years for camp-meeting purposes."[40] The upshot of what occurred as a result of finding the papers, and the way the county put down plans for a murderous insurrection revealed in the bundle, had historical precedent going back to 1874. At least, that was the basis of the argument used by those who did what they did in 1882; namely, they'd seen all this before! In 1874 a Black man named Huff Chaney (Cheney) told about some secret plans the Blacks in Choctaw County had, and that revelation got him brutally whipped by five Blacks. That's what led to a chaotic series of events that showcased weird alliances and, thus, weird betrayals, more dueling newspapers, and a world of extreme opinions, all of which is probably best understood by remembering that this was the "Reconstruction" era in Alabama and the years immediately after. Sources cited herein are largely those that came from white perspectives as is the narrative. For example, the following is the 1874 story line from the Montgomery newspaper, citing the *Choctaw Herald:* "The 'plans' which CHENEY divulged were certain preparations, then on foot among the blacks, 'to organize companies and seize the growing crops.' Four negroes had previously gone through Choctaw county telling the blacks that if they would do this, [President] GRANT would back them with troops in case the whites resisted the attempted robbery. These negroes said that they had been sent out from Mobile and New Orleans to have such companies organized, and that their advice was given by authority."[41] Those Blacks allegedly crossed over into neighboring Clarke and Wilcox Counties with the message that the president of the United States would back their bold plan. "In Wilcox they visited a 'colored' camp meeting, and after having told the preacher that their message to the people was of greater importance than his, took the stand and was proceeding to tell the colored troops all about Gen. GRANT'S purposes, when the old colored preacher, assisted by some of his congregation, interfered with their plans by arresting and sending them to the Wilcox jail." Note the reference to the Black congregants at the camp meeting as "colored troops." Whether that was said from the perspective of the four Blacks allegedly trying to recruit an army for their bold initiative, or whether that was a white attitude regarding every Black's potential threat, including religionists, isn't clear, but what was clear was the viewpoint of the *Wilcox Vindicator*, also cited in the article. The *Vindicator* was under the editorship of "Col. Charles L. Scott . . . a staunch and firm advocate of the rights of the South and for the constitutional liberty of the people North and South."[42] The Colonel had enlisted in the Confederate Army in April 1861 (as a "high private") with the 4th Alabama Regiment, and now, as editor of the *Vindicator*, he wasn't shy about what should be done with the alleged Black army recruiters: they should be handed over to federal authorities as "*black* Ku-Klux." Why, if the four Blacks had been white men they'd have been tried on federal charges of conspiracy against "*the negroes*" and, if found guilty, would have been sent to Albany Penitentiary for ten years. Instead, they were tried under Alabama statutes and got four-month sentences in the county jail. Thus opined Colonel Scott, quoted in the *Montgomery Advertiser.*

No pretenses are made here for telling the undisputed straight story regarding 1874 since that's impossible. There was too much emotion and vitriol and lack of objectivity from newspapers and otherwise, too many long-fixed customs and cultural norms to get all the ins and outs straight from 150 years ago. For example, some of the first reporting of what happened in Choctaw County indicated Huff Chaney was given some six hundred lashes by thirteen Blacks "for divulging some of the secrets of their secret organization."[43] Thereafter, Chaney went to Butler, the county seat, and swore out warrants against those who had beat him. The sheriff quickly arrested two of the assailants while four more resisted and escaped. Again, more war talk, more "army" terminology. "In a short time a band of 25 armed negroes assembled in Butler, and formed in line of battle, to rescue the two prisoners; four white citizens went to them to learn what they wanted. Their leader, a negro named Jack Turner, stated that the civil rights bill had passed; d——d if he didn't have his rights or die, and ordered his men to stand firm. The odds of 25 negroes to four whites made him brave, but fortunately at that moment a squad of white men rode into town; one shot was fired, and the colored troops retreated nobly." After the alleged incident in Butler the article noted "300 or 400 negroes collected on the Marengo [County] side" of the line near Tuscahoma, not far from a Choctaw County plantation, but dispersed upon learning that the sheriffs of Marengo and Choctaw Counties were raising men of their own in response.

"Another Radical Lie" is what the Choctaw County newspaper called an allegation by six Blacks, one of them the aforementioned Jack Turner, that whites had killed ten Blacks on August 13 at a political meeting at Turner's.[44] Jack Turner and five others signed a letter to W. B. Jones, the US Commissioner in Demopolis, which opened with a question: "Shall we colored Republicans be killed out again by the ku-klux?" The signers of the letter said they had to defend themselves when their "peaceful political meeting" was interrupted by pistol fire from the whites. Another question posed by the letter's signers: "The democrats say that not a radical shall vote in Choctaw in November. What shall we do?"

Insert the word "Republican" wherever the word "radical" appears, as in the Butler newspaper's calling out the allegations above as "a stinking Radical lie, manufactured by some white scoundrel with a black heart, for party purposes." The newspaper figured the Blacks listed as signatories weren't even aware of the letter that was sent; that the whole matter was about "creating a little party excitement, hoping to bring trouble upon the white people of this county." The local newspaper seemed to pin at least part of the blame on the editor of the "Republican," presumably the *Selma Republican*, which the Butler newspaper implied had advanced the lie by printing it. Butler was just a few miles from where the alleged massacre of the Blacks occurred; wouldn't you think the people of Butler would have heard about it, the local newspaper asked.

The Montgomery newspaper set out to show how Radical lies came to exist in Alabama, lies such as the alleged killing of ten Blacks. In doing that, the capital city newspaper asserted, it had what it referred to as a "written memorandum of JACK'S [Jack Turner's] confession, to a gentleman of this city," from which the newspaper compiled the following confessional statements:

> Huff Chaney had "betrayed some of our secrets to the white people"; that's what got him whipped and Jack Turner arrested;
>
> On the way to Butler to appear in court, Jack Turner collected all the Blacks he could—about two dozen armed men—and at a distance from the county seat encountered Whites coming to meet them;
>
> The Blacks took to the woods as the Whites fired some shots, Jack Turner saying he was shot at three times;
>
> Jack Turner went to Demopolis where he took a train to Montgomery as a delegate to the Republican State Convention, at which time he wasn't aware of anybody being killed;
>
> Turner helped to write the letter to the U.S. Commissioner stating that Blacks had been killed and did so in order to have Federal troops sent down to protect him for his role in whipping Huff Chaney.[45]

Again, the assertion that a white man was behind the writing of the letter was made. For what purpose? One word: "outrages"! It was a Republican conspiracy concocted for political effect, so that the radicals' "own worthless fingers may be kept in the Treasury and in the pockets of the people." Names, the Montgomery newspaper demanded: "Let us have the names of the *persons*!"[46] Naturally, names were not hard to come by, and the newspaper named its own list a couple of months later. For one it gave Charles Hays the distinction of being the "truly representative Southern Radical."[47] Hays, born in Greene County, had been a planter who owned a hundred slaves. When the Civil War broke out, he fought for the Confederacy but later became a Republican and US Congressman who advocated for the civil rights of Blacks. He was never forgiven by Democrats in Alabama for writing a letter in 1874 that was published on the front page of the *Hartford Daily Courant* in Connecticut, its editor a former Union general named Joseph R. Hawley, another name that would be smeared by Alabama Democrats thereafter. Hawley, telling Charles Hays in a letter that the people of the north were "both uninformed and misinformed" about what was going on in the South, asked the native Alabaman as a "gentleman of unimpeachable honor" to give a clear accounting of the outrages taking place.[48] Hays's sprawling, grim letter, which declared a "spirit of rebellion" existed "in the hearts of many misguided people" in Alabama, cited examples of an ongoing "reign of terror" in the state. He cited examples of killings and beatings of white Republicans and Blacks in Sumter, Russell, Macon, Coffee, Pickens, and Hale Counties. And in Choctaw County this account: "On or about the 1st of August the newspapers of Alabama were filled with the accounts of armed negroes congregating in Choctaw county for the purpose of commencing a war on the whites. Of course the excitement was intense. Hundreds of whites from different sections swiftly hurried to the scene of the supposed conflict, but when they arrived no fire armed [*sic*] negroes could be found. Yet something must be done to make an example. So a company of whites ambushed a party of negroes returning from church, killed ten and wounded thirteen." Congressman Charles Hays's letter of 1874 earned him the title of *scalawag* in his home state.[49] Likewise, whatever Reconstruction terminology could be applied to men could also pertain to newspapers that represented the political viewpoints of those men. *The Weekly State Journal*, or *Alabama Journal* as it was called, was given this assessment when it came into existence by its Montgomery competitor: "THE STATE JOURNAL—A new radical journal, published by C. T. Thweatt & Co., made its appearance this morning. It is neatly printed, but its politics is decidedly bad."[50] Within a few months of that notice C. T. Thweatt was part of a committee of five deemed "two Monkeys, two Hyenas and one Orangoutang [*sic*] with the Governor as the keeper" by the *Dadeville East Alabamian*, where Thweatt lived, this menagerie sent to Washington to request that more troops be sent to Alabama.[51] Thweatt's hometown newspaper said that he was elected to the "bogus Legislature" by thirteen white votes by a population of twenty thousand in this county and that the "so-called negro Legislature of Alabama" had slandered the state by asking for more military troops when "Law and order prevails here." Little wonder the *State Journal* policy regarding correspondence included this caveat: "Personally abusive articles will not be inserted on any terms."[52] The *State Journal* remained a Democratic whipping boy even after C. T. Thweatt left the newspaper. "Please, Mr. radical editor, don't hurt us. We'll be good boys and do as you say. Will you be so kind and condescending as to let us choose whether we will associate with carpetbaggers or with the negroes? . . . We only beg this favor because some of us if forced to make a choice, much prefer to associate with decent negroes."[53] Carpetbaggers? Why, they're "generally vagrants having no visible means of support. They live solely on politics." The decent Blacks, however, worked for a living and were good citizens. Still, if some might choose a decent Black over a scurrilous white carpetbagger, the position of the "Executive Committee of the Democratic and Conservative Party of Alabama" was accompanied by a racial formula. In staking out its statewide political position in the turbulent year of 1874 by means of four points, the meat of the matter was in these two:

> 2d. That the Republican or Radical party in Alabama is composed of about nine-tenths negroes and one-tenth whites.
>
> 3d. That the Democratic and Conservative Party is composed almost exclusively of the white people of the State embracing a majority of the people.[54]

The Republican Party "North, East and West" might have respectable people within its ranks, people "dictated by an honest judgment and true patriotic feeling," but it was different in Alabama. "The negroes, forming nine-tenths of the party here, are of course as a body ignorant, and from their recent condition of slavery a low order of morality prevails among them." The rest of the party was mostly "professional politicians and their hangers-on" who had no qualms about stealing and lying. Those men of low character would have the president of the United States believe that a "new rebellion" was brewing, and it was no surprise that Charles Hays, General Hawley, and the *State Journal* were singled out in connection with the allegations.

To get to the truth would have required a veritable Pickett's Charge headlong into withering allegations, conflicting statements, conspiracies, charges and countercharges, political posturing and maneuvering; that's what 1874 was! So, in 1882, when Choctaw County officials said they did what they did because they had encountered something similar in 1874, what was their meaning? In 1882, 1874 was recalled as "armed resistance to arrest" when county officials offered a defense for their actions against Jack Turner to Gov. R. W. Cobb.[55] What was actually involved in what took place is speculation, but between September 26, 1874, when Jack Turner had a newspaper article read to him and allegedly put his "mark" ("X") on a statement saying he knew nothing about any Black churchgoers being killed and wounded in Choctaw County,[56] and on August 15, 1882, when the white boy allegedly found the bundle of secret papers, Blacks, to their own detriment as it turned out, were seemingly able to read and write and set down in detail rebellious, secret, and murderous plans against whites. The following was referred to as secret "Paper No. 4" from the bundle allegedly found on the roadside:

> this is our last meeting this sid of our time and we only have 23 member in desotoville Precinct and we are going to take this county by sheding Blood and we are going to slay From the Young Up to the oldest and Capt Jack turner is Going with his mens that night to Battle and Capt Moses turner will go up to the Camp Grown and Capt. Peter Hill will take his men to Desotoville and Capt. Jesy Wilson will take his men to Mt. Sterling and you all must look out and be taking and we will meet on the 17 night of Sept. For this will be our time when every Body will have Preaching in minds.

> Mr. turner is our Gen. and when we take this county we will Pay him[.] Mr. F. D. Barney is our Book keeper we will Pay him too.

On August 19, 1882, Jack Turner, the alleged "General" of a Black army, was lynched in Butler by a mixed crowd of whites and Blacks estimated at a thousand people. He was removed from jail and "taken to a tree near the court house and formally executed."[57] It was nearing camp-meeting season in Choctaw County, and, based on what those secret papers purportedly revealed, Jack Turner planned to massacre unarmed white men, women, and children on the campgrounds. Jack Turner was deemed the "life and soul" of the conspiracy. The best way to "disorganize the conspiracy"? That would be the death of the one man responsible, said the local newspaper in defense mode a couple of weeks later. The hanging was a day—an occasion—for waxing eloquent: "If they could have beheld the expressions of relief and gratitude depicted on the faces of some of Butler's fair daughters, that the outlaw and desperate man Jack Turner, had been caused to pass to 'that bourne from whence no traveler ere, returns,' after runing [*sic*] for so many long years a terror to our people; they would have hung their heads in silence and heartily said amen to the action taken on that day."[58] The hanging was "a green spot in the hearts [of] the women and children of our county!" according to the letter writer signed "Tompkins Bluff," who traveled to Butler the day of the lynching and felt it should be remembered in reverential terms, with heads bowed in thankfulness and hearty amens, not unlike camp-meeting style. The men responsible for hanging Jack Turner pretty much checked all the boxes where Christian character was concerned, at least according to Tompkins: "And when I remember the names and characters of the men who engaged in it; men whose hearts glow with every manly instinct, men who have never been known to turn a human from their doors hungry, men whose voices have ever been lifted in defence [*sic*] of the weak and unprotected, I feel that I would be recreant to my God, my country and my people if I failed to endorse in this public manner, the action of that day." The men who took the law into their hands were, based on the description, no different from men who attended camp meetings; men who were the backbone of the institution. It's not difficult to imagine them camping when the next opportunity arose following the hanging. Another letter writer—"East Oaktuppa"—noted this reaction from what transpired: "The negro war has demolished the camp meeting, and numbers of our ladies have not yet gotten over the scare. Such things are unfortunate, but cant [*sic*] be helped under the circumstances."[59]

There was no end to embellishments in the aftermath of the hanging, no lack of twists and turns that emerged. "NO MERCY" was what one "correspondent from a distant point" said was to be on the black flag that was to be raised over the white camp meeting by the general's marauding troops. Even the local paper allowed for the possibility that it might be hearsay. Jack Turner's army or "club" was said to include as many as four hundred Blacks when the story of the Butler hanging was picked up by other newspapers; it was described as an army with powder and shot and eight hundred guns in its arsenal.[60] For eight years Jack had been Choctaw County's *bête noir* [*sic*]—black beast—who had "met his death cooly"; "died persisting in a stubborn denial of the charges contained in the papers." Another newspaper: Jack Turner, "a turbulent and dangerous character, a regular firebrand in the community," was hung around 1:15 p.m., "swung in mid-air" for eight and a half minutes, and the rope cut at 1:30 p.m.[61] The Butler newspaper carried a dramatic and macabre account from the *Meridian Mercury* in Mississippi:

> The condemned man's hands were tied behind him, and his feet lashed together. Others went and got a buggy. Jack was made to mount up into it, and to give the regulation fall a chair was put into the bottom of the buggy and stood up into it. The hangman's noose was decently adjusted, and time given for prayer. Jack did the praying for himself, and prayed eloquently to God, for Christ's sake, that moment to receive his soul in Heaven. The buggy moved from its place and Jack Turner dropped several feet. His feet touched the ground from the stretch of the rope. Men quickly mounted the tree, untied the rope, and heavy, strong men pulled on the end of it and raised the limp, dangling form a little so that it could swing more comfortably. It is believed the precaution was needless, as it is thought the neck was broken by the fall, and instantaneous death ensued.[62]

It was said Jack Turner had but two last requests: that he be buried "decently" at Mount Sterling and that his wife be allowed to come to him and kiss him one more time. The hanging committee waited for a while, but when Jack's wife couldn't be found, "Jack had to go without the last tender kiss."

Jack's "leading squads" were to go to Butler, Mount Sterling, Desotoville, and elsewhere and kill all whites—"people . . . at camp-meeting, unarmed, and could then offer no resistance." The bundle of papers found—that trove of Black insurrection plans? Well, what the Blacks planned "outstripped anything in Indian annals" and "proved to be the minutes of a negro organization formed for the virtual extinguishment of the white population and Democratic negroes in that county."[63] Even with the man dead, his methods were said to be spreading to other counties, requiring people to "keep their eyes open."[64] In that regard, it was an odd note the Butler newspaper addressed "To the Greenville Advocate" "The description of 'Little John White,' except as to color, is altogether unsuited to Jack Turner, who was a very large man, 6 ft. 1 or 2 in. in height, and weighed over 200 lbs. He did not wear beads, and dressed plainly."[65] It sounded much like a hanging yet to come at that point, the one regarding Tom Barsh in 1903, and the white superstition regarding the large Black man who could live on after being lynched, his terror and evil-doing surviving even the gallows. Confusion and superstition regarding Jack Turner's evil nature had apparently made its way to Butler County, as it had to other places where ongoing vigilance was required by men who were guardians of the southern way, much like the heroic boys in gray had done twenty years earlier, their ghosts still restless and unsatisfied.

Truth was, those heroic boys in gray lived on in post–Civil War groups like the Conecuh Guards out of Greenville, Gulf City Guards out of Mobile, Pollard Light Guards out of Pollard, Herbert Light Infantry out of Geneva, and Troy Rifles out of Troy. In the Reverend Fendley's home county, Wilcox, the Wilcox Mounted Rifles were constantly drilling, pleading for uniforms and an armory, and bivouacking and camping with the Tuscaloosa Warrior Guards and other protectors like those named above. Why? To stay battle ready for incidents precisely like those surrounding the alleged camp-meeting massacre;

to prevent unholy Black brutes from falling upon white defenseless, holy campers. *Vigilance* was the operative word. That was needed more than ever in the dangerous world in between the Civil War and an ill-defined future. Disciplined protectors of the social order were needed to preserve the majesty and dignity of an old system that produced chivalrous young men. That's purportedly why the Wilcox Mounted Rifles were founded in 1888, or, for perspective, between the hanging of Jack Turner in Choctaw County in 1882, and Fred Kidd's hanging in Grove Hill, witnessed by the reverend, in 1890. Little wonder that the mere sight of the Wilcox Mounted Rifles must have stirred the hopes and stanched the flow of fears of the women folk. Everyone was looking out for the Wilcox Mountain Rifles: the pretty girls that attended social events, like the "lawn party" that drew two hundred guests when the gallant young men honored "visiting young ladies,"[66] or the bevy of beauties—"more beautiful young girls . . . than at any similar entertainment"—that attended any "Rifles' ball" and watched the gallant Rifles target shoot in manly competition for a box of cigars, then danced into the "wee sma' hours," the way they did on that occasion at the Ellis Plantation, a few miles outside county-seat Camden.[67] Perhaps *imagination* was the key here, the way the *idea* of the camp meeting appealed to some in spite of the real-world, uneasy associations with camping for Jesus. Both were a fleeting return to the balance and equilibrium associated with the past. Regarding the Rifles, it wasn't only the young girls smitten by their manly presence; so too were the older ladies, like those of Possum Bend, who prepared an "elegant dinner" between Rock West and Oak Lawn churches to benefit the Rifles, who showed their thanks by drilling for the crowd.[68] (They were always drilling in preparation for the next conflagration!) Indeed, it was the matrons of the "Alabama Charter" Chapter of the United Daughters of the Confederacy that came into being on March 26, 1896, precisely on behalf of the Rifles.[69] On into the twentieth century, the Rifles were the star attraction at parades in places like Pine Hill, where thirty-nine Rifles pitched camp on the Camden side of Southern Railroad "in true military style."[70] On horseback, drilling in preparation for a nameless enemy—any enemy!—the Wilcox Mounted Rifles signaled security in a changing world fraught with uncertainty and danger. The Rifles were a vestige from a not-so-distant past when the world wasn't topsy-turvy. There could be no such thing as "at ease" in the in-between world. Somebody stated the case: "The necessity that compels a standing army or citizen soldierly is more strongly felt among lawless and poverty ridden people. In sections where want and misery are likely to force the people to desperate deeds in order to secure the means of sustenance the militia and police is largely more numerous than where sufficiency reigns. The efficacy and promptness of the response and activity of the troops depends on the support or aid given by the people of the community."[71] Why, there were still crimes as yet unsolved—like the "two acts of incendiarism without a parallel in the history of Alabama" that nearly burned down the county seat.[72] At least, nobody had been brought to justice when the letter writer laid the whole kit and caboodle—Camden ablaze in the dead of night at three points, thirty buildings destroyed—at the feet of "carpet-bag incapacity" and inability to protect life, liberty, and property. That's why the Wilcox Mounted Rifles were needed; that's why people raised hell and resisted the plan after the first decade of the twentieth century to absorb the Rifles into the National Guard. The enemy was still out there, ready to start new fires and commit new crimes; enemies like Jack Turner over in Choctaw County!

County officials, in justifying the hanging death of Jack Turner, published a list of his past crimes and transgressions that received wide coverage. Besides charges related to the lynching of Huff Chaney, Jack's alleged criminal history included living in adultery, disturbing females at assembly, defacing the jail while incarcerated, assault and battery with a stick, gambling, disturbing religious worship, all of which made him "a walking menace in the community."[73]

The other side in the Jack Turner hanging had a different perspective regarding the man and his death. Those secret papers allegedly found by a white boy were elsewhere declared to have been found by "two gentlemen"[74] and by a Choctaw County "Greenbacker,"[75] the Greenbackers being a post–Civil War party that opposed the reduction of paper money in circulation. Perhaps the white boy's father was a Greenbacker, and the father told another Greenbacker about his son's discovery and that constituted the "two gentlemen" credited with finding the plans for a camp-meeting massacre. And perhaps that was one of the alliances strained by the Jack Turner hanging, since it was noted that there existed a "coalition between the Greenbackers and Republicans."[76] Whatever, the Mobile *Gazette*, a Republican paper edited by a Black man, Phillip Joseph, would have none of the Choctaw County allegations regarding Jack Turner.[77] It said the hanging resulted because "a colored republican of Choctaw county," namely, Jack Turner, made Choctaw one of five Alabama counties to prevail against Democrats in the last election. So terror-stricken were the Democrats "that they devised a scheme by which a certain manuscript should be found purporting to be a record of the meeting of a colored organization, at the head of which [Jack Turner] was. . . . They arrested him and six other colored men, tortured one of them by the lash, till he confessed that he wrote the manuscript, then read it before an assembled multitude of 700 people at the court house, all but 200 of whom voted that Jack Turner should be taken out of jail and hung." From this perspective, a martyr, that's what Jack Turner had become, and the hanging in Butler on August 15, 1882, was deemed by the *Gazette* the worst outrage against democracy ever perpetrated in a southern state.

That view was seconded by George Turner, a white lawyer in Montgomery and chairman of the Republican Executive Committee of Alabama, or, as the Democrats referred to him, "The Champion Liar of Alabama."[78] George Turner linked Choctaw County to a troubled matrix of racial violence: Choctaw was south of Sumter County, Alabama, and Sumter County was across the state line from Kemper County, Mississippi. Congressman Charles Hays in 1874, in that scathing letter printed in northern newspapers, identified Sumter County as the place where a young lawyer named Walter P. Billings had been murdered at Ramsey after addressing a Republican meeting—"He was literally shot to pieces," his wife said[79]—and a Black government mail agent named Thomas Ivey was ambushed and killed when somebody flagged the train down on which he was riding. Kemper County, a place rife with racial violence in those days, was where the "Chisolm massacre" had occurred. In 1875, Judge William Chisolm, a Republican, was accused in the shooting death of a Democratic Party candidate for sheriff and was in jail in protective custody with members of his family and some Republican friends. A mob of hundreds stormed the jail and killed Chisolm and his son and some of the judge's friends. George Turner, in referring to the Jack Turner lynching in Butler, was quoted saying Choctaw's proximity to Sumter and Kemper Counties offered insight into the "character and disposition" of the people who hung Jack Turner. "[I]n pleasant company," he said facetiously. "I knew Jack Turner personally very well. He is said to have been the ringleader. He was a very large and powerfully built black man, without any education, but gifted with great force of character. The people of his race in that county had great confidence in him. He was born a slave about 36 or 40 years ago, of pure negro blood, with a perfectly black skin, and was freed by the war. He had worked hard, got some money together, bought a place for himself and had it well stocked, and was regarded as one of the well-to-do farmers in the county. He was also a local preacher a thoroughly good man, and was known as 'the Rev. Jack Turner.' I have no idea in the world that he was connected with any conspiracy to kill the whites or that there was any such conspiracy." According to George Turner, since the end of the Civil War there hadn't been a known case of Blacks conspiring to kill whites and the Choctaw County debacle was "laughed at as absurd" by Blacks.

What George Turner felt was behind Jack Turner's hanging was an incident involving a Choctaw County cotton planter named Carnathan. The planter worked a couple of hundred Blacks on his plantation and directed them to vote Democratic in elections. In November 1880, when one of those Black men, William Manning, refused to follow Carnathan's order regarding voting, the planter whipped Manning with what George Turner described as "a heavy leathern mule trace, having an iron hitching hook on the end of it." Two months after the whipping, January 1881, George Turner said he saw William Manning in court in Mobile, his back and shoulders with "open, running sores" from the beating. Jack Turner, along with William Manning and others, testified before a grand jury against Carnathan for voter coercion, and the planter was indicted. As a result of his testimony, Jack Turner told George Turner of his fears of violence, and the latter told him to arm himself. That testimony against the cotton planter, plus the fact Jack Turner was chairman of the Choctaw County Republican Committee, which missed carrying the county ticket by a couple of dozen votes, led

George Turner to conclude these circumstances led to the arrests of Jack Turner and of his alleged "captains" and to Turner's hanging. The alleged conspiracy regarding the camp-meeting killing? According to George Turner, "The colored people of Choctaw are not great hands at writing, and are not likely to have many papers on their meetings except those of a very simple character, and it would not be a difficult matter to forge such papers as a pretext to arouse the passions of bad, violent men, and so get rid of Turner."[80]

Camp meetings, with all their praying and shouting and ecstatic dancing and holy laughter, were powerless against such fixed social and cultural courses as those cut by institutionalized slavery and the Industrial Revolution in America. Sarah Maria Cornell, the young factory worker, was a cog in a world of powered machinery in 1830s New England. She was one of many young women enticed to leave a rural area for reasons personal and economic and come to cities to work in factories and make their way in a brave new world. Those young women would learn difficult lessons in those textile factories but also learn to fight for their rights against powerful men. Black slaves weren't so much cogs as they were human machines. Eli Whitney's cotton gin only made it necessary and more profitable for powerful men to have more human machines in play. Thus, Sarah Maria Cornell, Jack Turner, William Manning, and Thomas Ivey shared similar fates with regard to the camp meeting, namely, the high probability that not many campers invoked the Almighty to intercede on their behalf as representatives of the sexually and racially abused. Campers took their politics and preconceived notions camping with them, so it was reasonable in that day to blame a morally corrupt woman, not a Methodist preacher, and a big, burly freedman, not a white righteous mob. Praying in the pine straw was ultimately all about preserving the status quo and the world's equilibrium. Plus, religion in Alabama has always been about not necessarily finding peace, but the next foe or enemy—the next demon or monster threatening the commonwealth. Fixated as campers were on salvation and finding Jesus, few probably paid attention to the Gospel account regarding the Savior meeting the Gadarene demoniac outside the city, in the wilderness, where camping brought Alabamans face to face with their fears, some of which were simply too world shattering to confront.

A few years before the twentieth century's arrival, Alabamans were still in the thrall that had resulted in the Jack Turner lynching in 1882. Whether the state is freed from that bondsman yet is a legitimate question that needs to be asked. In 1897 the familiar headline was "Race War Imminent."[81] Where? Etowah County—Sand Mountain, the other end of the state from Butler and Choctaw County. The reporting had all the elements that have appeared in the preceding pages: race, sex, religion, wild camp-meeting type expressions. A Black woman, it seemed, had taken up preaching on Sand Mountain. Her congregants were "negroes and ignorant whites." She claimed to be the Messiah, complete with miracles. There was a big foot washing, and the Blacks and whites "intermingled freely, embracing each other with the 'holy kiss.'" When the alleged Black Woman Messiah allegedly cursed a prominent white citizen she came across, he allegedly "cowhided her within an inch of her life. . . . Her followers swear they will exterminate the better element of the white people and a clash may come at any time. She has laid several plots to bushwhack those who have persuaded her to desist." So many *alleged* and *allegedly!* That's because, even by 1897, the Sand Mountain story bore watching, the reporting newspaper said, but added in a subhead, "if True."

# Conclusion

## Two Men Squabble

It strikes me that the Reverend Fendley in 1905 wasn't exactly keen about all things past. Concerning his boyhood days, he remembered this:

> In those days many houses were built with no blocks, dirt floors, one door, no windows. Bedsteads were mostly homemade, many of them only one leg. Stools served as chairs, cooking utensils were generally an oven skillet with a handle, a frying pan, a pot, a gourd for milking, a soap and lard gourd, tin cups and plates, flint and powder for getting fires. Rarely any table cloth. Coffee for breakfast and biscuits only on Sunday morning. Farming tools were a scooter [a type of plough perhaps?], shovel, weeding hoe, a two wheeled cart or slide for hauling, reap hook for oats and wheat, mortar and pedles [*sic*] for cleaning rough rice, hand mills for grinding corn, cards for carding cotton, spinning wheels, reels, warping bars and looms for making cloth, troughs for tanning leather, a shoe knife and hammer, maple pegs for making shoes. For dances the music instruments were a tin pan, a gourd fiddle, fife, flute, three bones and a patter ["bones," wood pieces held between the fingers and clicked together?; "patter," pieces of wood struck in percussive manner?]. There were no wash pans, when one wanted to wash feet, hands and face, one poured the water while the person did the washing. I have poured the water often times. I have known men who owned a horse for a year without a saddle. I have held many a torch at the table while the rest were eating. No such thing as a gate or forder. Log rolling and house raising was all done by the neighbors.

Throw in no ladies' hats, only bonnets, no buggies, no pianos or organs, no guitars; no bureaus or dressers, no clocks, no stoves, no railroads, no steam mills, and no blind tigers (places where illegal liquor was sold—he was probably okay with that). Still, he referred to those days as "comparatively speaking, a free country."

For the purpose of highlighting the sometime wild and wooly nature of camp-meeting religion and the dash of spiritual "Tabasco" by which open-air religion spiced up everyday church life, sometimes to its detriment, uneasiness, and shame, we can allude to a third "religion" of sorts; one that in all likelihood would have excluded the reverend, and one in which he would likely have declined membership. In his native Wilcox County, during the time he was planting churches in neighboring Clarke County, there existed a rather high-toned secret society of sorts. "Our Circle" was, frankly, as hard to understand as it was to join. Actually, one had to be born into it.

Our Circle considered itself charming and those who thought differently were reminded of the fable of the fox and grapes.[1] It was simply sour grapes to point out the Olympian smugness behind their funny talk, funny names, poem quoting, and debates on weird subjects, such as "Does Civilization Increase Happiness?"[2] Two points about Our Circle: They always met in resplendent, flower-strewn settings and, unlike the poor camp meeting, weather always favored them and existed to serve their classical whims. Yes, even nature bowed to the intellect and elegance of the membership, its playfulness and impudence. Since it was the final meeting of the year for Our Circle, the song that followed the oration was "The Last Rose of Summer" by "Miss Mary M.," and "Mignonette," one of Our Circle's refined but flamboyant scribes concluded, "hence Our Circle would hibernate until the fields again laughingly appear, the flowers put forth their smiling faces, trees bud and birds carol merrily, announcing the approach of spring. . . . Nature then teaching beauty, truth, love and melody."[3]

It was that kind of falderal, play-acting, a kind of living theater. It was as if members of the royalty, if not gods and goddesses, were flitting about Cedar Grove at the "palatial residence of Mrs. M. Burford" when the self-styled "literary institution" that was Our Circle met there.[4] "Around the fireside there was friendly conversation; the drawing room brilliantly illuminated and adorned with fragrant flowers, fair women and chivalry; each radient [*sic*] countenance showing the interest manifested as they discussed 'Our Circle' and the pleasure in anticipation." They couldn't get enough of themselves. The "Presidential chair" occupied by Sol D. Bloch, "gentleman, generous, brave, and an ardent admirer of the fair sex." Miss Flora Murphy, "crowned Vice President": "Beauty, grace and a merry heart she has." W. P. Burford, secretary: "This knight we commend for his modesty, valor, intellect, constancy and affection, 'Veni, vidi, vici.'" (The Latin, attributed to Julius Caesar, means "I came, I saw, I conquered.") Miss Ruby Gullette, "an amiable, sympathetic and handsome brunette, accepting with a smiling face the irksome task of guarding the overflowing coffers of Our Circle."

Again, the reverend, born in that very county in 1836 on Cub Creek, probably didn't have the bloodline or credentials to be a classicist like the gauzy, spectral women and refined, intellectual knights of the Our Circle lot, floating through old-world plantation homes looking for something just as surely as the Wilcox Mounted Rifles, their contemporaries, were. It's hard to imagine Our Circle sitting through an "oration" by the reverend on faithful church membership or what constituted a missionary Baptist church. Likewise, he would likely have rejected them because of the cloaked sexuality at play in their sophisticated meetings. Sure, it was a tease, like Our Circle in general. Mr. Luck Jenkins's talk on "The Society Belle," deemed "a very graphic description of 'the girl of the period,'" probably evoked titters and eye rolls from the women, but he was merely countering Miss Flora's matrimonial assessment of the young men of the day.[5] Likewise, when Judge Starr read a poem, "Wooing a Hundred Years Hence," somebody asked His Honor if the reason he was originating a new method of love making was because he had failed at the present one. It was all in good fun, but likely not the kind of fun the reverend would have found comfortable. Still, way down deep, in spite of its classical bent and posturing, Our Circle was no different from the run of the mill.

> A reading by Miss Millie Mangham—"The Rev. Knack O. Strong." 'Twas read in the strain or brogue peculiar to the negro, and reflects much credit upon one so young.

"Stealing a Green Watermillion," by Miss Mary Murphy, another rendition of "ni**erism," was well recited.[6]

The camp meeting, Mounted Rifles, and Our Circle had something in common. All were afraid of the future. All three were trying to hold on for all they were worth against time, which cared not for barking and jerking, constant drilling and target shooting, and pretentious classical meanderings reminiscent of antebellum times.

I suspect the two of us, the reverend and I, would hold different views regarding what these pages represent. For him, he might caution me against the dangers of "rambling," a word encountered often back in the old days that seemed to define a free-spirited jaunt, carefree, just to see what you could see. You know, checking things out. A possum hunt could be a ramble and was for him on an occasion. As a boy, he and some chums grabbed a torch, got their faithful dog, and set off in the dark. In no time they were lost and started, as he put it, to "hollo." He "holloed" for his "Pap and Mer," as he put it—Pop and Mom. As it turned out, the fearless boy hunters were within fifty steps of the front yard; Pap heard them and asked what the matter was. The reverend went in and scrunched down in a corner by the fireplace, humiliated, Pap and Mer laughing. The reverend might say a ramble through an Alabama camp-meeting site could have unintended consequences, too; that I could end up in a corner like him on that occasion, smarting from my attempt to act like something I'm not. And, of course, he might consider it tampering with "holy" things to point out the all-too-human side of camp meetings. To him, in camping terms, I could reply that the nearly hundred years since he died have seen no abatement whatsoever in the world's desire to rush in with noise and corruption when the pure of heart seek a wilderness place to commune with the Spirit. I could say those "tents of distraction" have only spread like wildfire; that everybody shops there today, skipping preaching to do so; that "campers" have given up their pilgrim tents, so easily struck, for permanent structures that witness to the fact we're here to stay, as much a part of this world as the next—actually, barely cognizant of any "next." As a man of ardent, heaven-minded religion, the reverend might be shocked to see how little of what he spent a lifetime preaching is in play today; how little of it survived, stolen away by that horse-thief time, which also made off with what little discernment there was to begin with. Jesus! The camp-meeting idea is overrun by politicians today, glad-handing and back-slapping, and testifying to their support of some idyllic, archetype camp meeting, and what that fairy tale allegedly stood for!

It's not as if I think I could prevail over the reverend in a debate. Quite to the contrary. When he died on January 20, 1927, this was said about him in the newspaper, which, alas, filled in gaps he never got around to in telling his own story: "He was a man of limited education but was endowed with a brilliant mind and was recognized as a man of unusual ability."[7] That native ability is no small thing, so I have no desire to pick religious fights with the fellow who occasionally bangs the pots and pans in my soul house. Rather, I live in peace with the fact that we have differences of opinion. At the beginning of his "Sixty Nine Years in the World" the reverend noted that he had no recollections about certain childhood "firsts" (first word, first recollection of father and mother, and so on); that those "are all a dark place in my life." But childhood firsts lost in a dark place in the memory are not the same as willful blindness or shocking lack of discernment in an adult. For example, take the reverend's recollection concerning one Mr. L. D. Godbolt, a plantation owner with whom he boarded as a schoolboy. The reverend referred to him as a "Christian gentleman." Mr. "Christian" Godbolt had quite a number of slaves and a slave overseer that worked them and made the plantation profitable. L. D. Godbolt seemed to be a kind of "Job" character for the reverend. He had all the blessings: a fertile plantation and the slaves to work it; a "pious wife"; good-looking daughters, one of which, "Miss Mary," was a knockout; and he was charitable toward the reverend. As for me, anytime I hear descriptions like "Christian gentleman," "good Christian," or any combination of "Christian" linked with a businessman, politician, teacher, judge, counselor, doctor, police officer, financier, etc., alarm bells go off, and I'm immediately wary. Call me a skeptic, or call me discerning, but I want to know what "Christian" means in that context, since, if you can be a Christian slaveowner, well, you can pretty much say "Christian" to anything or anybody. The reverend could talk about his father buying "his first negro" in the same factual, unruffled manner that he mentioned his father shot a turkey, or hitched up the oxen and moved his family to a new location. It was just life in the South in those days. The reverend would remember that somewhere around 1857, he became "lawfully a free man," a big deal since, in his nineteenth-century estimation, the "fair sect [sex] thinks more of a man than anything else on earth." Yet, much of his ministry was during the post-Reconstruction era, followed by the Jim Crow era, when "Christians" did everything to thwart Blacks from being just that "free men." Did the reverend advocate for the Christian rights and civil liberties of former slaves? I honestly have no idea, only suspicions regarding that. Let's just say I'm grateful that there was reporting on him mounting a scaffold to pray for a Black man being hanged for murder, as opposed to those who said the hanging—lynching—of another Black man was a Christian act performed by Christian men. Me, I'll take what I can from history, and that includes the camp meeting.

Together and individually the reverend and I are the essence of what it means to be human: mixed-up, at odds with self, mistake-ridden, blind to consequences, and trying to figure the whole thing out. The reverend reminds me to laugh at life's absurdities rather than be confounded by them; reminds me that, yes, tragedy is at the heart of life and existence, but equally so is slapstick where, in this comedy of errors, we go to church, or the holy place, all dressed up in outlandish garments, thinking all the while what a fine figure we cut! God, on the other hand, sees our dirty knees scrubbed red, our overstuffed pants with the strained galluses, the tacky calico gown and borrowed hat, and must give a holy laugh at the sight of such foolishness, that is, when He isn't royally pissed about everything. I like to think the reverend did the best he could under the circumstances, like some of those at camp meeting, in maneuvering the theater of operations that is the individual's lifespan. Calling it a combat zone probably isn't an exaggeration! That the reverend ended up a Christian soldier after being a Rebel one seems to me a conclusion far better than what might have been, one I can live with and do.

# Notes

## Chapter 1

1. "Freak Cults Under Name Of Religion," by Alfred W. Greeley, *Birmingham News*, Feb. 23, 1907, 10; unless otherwise noted, the newspapers cited were published in Alabama. The article by Greeley appeared in other newspapers across the country as well.

2. "Gluck Colonists Are Like Shadows," *Chicago Tribune*, Aug. 28, 1907, 3.

3. "'Chief Architect' of New Race Here," *New York Times*, Aug. 28, 1907, 16.

4. "'Chief Architect,'" 16. The prerequisites for becoming a Gluckite included no alcohol, no meat, no smoking, and good morals. Concerning the group's desire to develop human's twelve senses, those were identified by the chief architect as "seeing, hearing, smelling, tasting, touching, feeling, intuition, transmission of ideas, telepathy, spiritual discernment, clear sight, and realization."

5. "Adamless Eden," *Houston Post* (TX), Dec. 20, 1906, 14.

6. "'Brute' Man Is Shut Out," *Brownsville Herald* (TX), Dec. 5, 1906, 2. The other quotations in this paragraph come from this source.

7. "New York Town Talk," *Central New Jersey Home News* (New Brunswick, NJ), Jan. 22, 1907, 7. "Many prominent persons in this city joined together to establish this hotel for women. The idea was philanthropic in that it was planned to give a pleasant home and a chance for social intercourse at moderate cost to women who worked for a livelihood and who because they have no relatives or come from afar are compelled to live in boarding houses. There was no idea of making the hotel a charity." Clean sheets and good intentions notwithstanding, prices were going up, stockholders weren't making anything off the hotel, plus the Martha Washington property had doubled in value at the same time the hotel struggled—well, a turn to money-making was called for and the original idea was scrapped.

8. "To Bar Men from Trinity's Pulpit," *Trenton Evening News* (NJ), Aug. 7, 1909, 12.

9. "The Old Camp-Meeting Days—William Arnold," by W. F. Samford,

LLD, in *Wesleyan Christian Advocate*, *The Tuskegee News*, Oct. 9, 1884, 1. The quotation right after this one in the text comes from the same source.

10. Eben E. Rexford, "The Swamp Secret—A Story of the Frontier (Chapters XIX and XX)," *Centreville Press*, June 18, 1900, 3.

11. The First Great Awakening is regarded as the revival that swept Great Britain and the thirteen American colonies during the eighteenth century.

12. "'Old Cane Ridge,'" *Courier-Journal* (Louisville, KY), Sept. 13, 1903, 39. Regarding the richest land in Kentucky, Boone said, "Heaviest cane, tallest corn, most game, abound on Cane Ridge, and, from the growth of sugar trees, I think it has the richest soil."

13. "'Old Cane Ridge,'" 39. The article noted that later on physicians would attribute the jerks, barking, laughing and such as expressions of "nervous excitement," while hypnotists would consider them "the wonderful effects of suggestion." Greeley, however, referred to "marvelous tales" where "scoffers and cynics, particularly physicians, . . . were attacked by retributive 'jerks' and bounced and dashed about until they cried for mercy and were converted."

14. W. H. Purvis, "A Kentucky Revival Meeting," *Courier-Journal*, originally appeared in the *American Magazine*, Sept. 25, 1887, 13.

15. "Beating Fanaticism out of a Man," *Rutland Weekly Herald* (VT), Oct. 8, 1846, 1. "Wm. Dorrill" died in 1846 at the age of ninety-four. He was remembered in part because of an assertion he made one time before his followers, namely, "no arm can hurt my flesh." At that point, Ezekiel Foster, who was on hand as a "spectator," got up and proceeded to throttle the cult leader. Foster was described as a "man of good sense, of a giant frame, and had a countenance that bespoke authority." Apparently, "indignant" also described Foster as regarded Dorrill's claim to "mysterious powers." The beating seems to have sent Dorrill packing.

16. Presumably a reference to the musket.

17. "Camp Meeting," *Brewton Banner*, July 7, 1883, 2. The first two quotations in the next paragraph are from the same source.

18. "Big Camp-Meeting at Little Texas," *Times-Argus*, Aug. 28, 1885, 1. All of the quotations attributed to letter writer in the following paragraphs come from this source.

19. Hermits or recluses.

20. "The Camp Meeting," *Tuskegee News*, Aug. 30, 1877, 3. The quotations in the following paragraph are from the same source.

21. "Culpepper Pranks," *Montgomery Advertiser*, May 30, 1904, 4.

22. "Camp Meetings," taken from the *New York Times*, *Sunday Magazine*,

in *Brewton Standard*, Nov. 17, 1932, 4. The quotations in this paragraph come from the same source.

23. "Birth of Christian Church at Historic 'Cane Ridge Meeting House' Is Recalled in Memorial Services for James Rogers," *Lexington Herald* (Lexington, KY), May 29, 1921, 2.

24. "Cane Ridge," *Blue-Grass Blade* (Lexington, KY), Oct. 25, 1903, 1.

25. "Many Attend Opening Of Camp Nikelojo," *Clarke County Democrat* (Grove Hill), July 14, 1927, 3.

26. Barkley was a salesman, reportedly a bystander at the whipping, when he "was shot through the heart." The story as reported involved threats of killing white people, whites whipping Blacks, a mob manhunt, bloodhounds, "negroes . . . badly beaten up to extort information," a reward, and ultimately the deaths of two men, one white and one Black. See "J. M. Barkley Killed Monday Night," *Democrat-Reporter* (Linden), July 1, 1926, 1.

27. "Letter to Club Members," *Democrat Reporter* (Linden), July 1, 1926, 1.

28. "Agent Outlines Work of Conservation Corps," *Clarke County Democrat*, May 13, 1937, 1.

29. "SONGS, One Cent Each," advertisement, *Clarke County Democrat*, Mar. 16, 1882, 3.

30. "Community Center Is Nearing Completion," *Clarke County Democrat*, July 25, 1940, 1. The next two quotations are from the same source.

31. "4-H Club Girls to Camp at Suggsville," *Clarke County Democrat*, June 30, 1949, 1.

32. "Clarke County Baptists Plan Boy's Camp Soon," *Clarke County Democrat*, July 28, 1955, 8.

33. "Sunbeam Day Camp at Camp Morvin," *Clarke County Democrat*, Aug. 10, 1961, 3.

34. "Rev. Paul Smith to Speak at Youth Retreat," *Clarke County Democrat*, Aug. 24, 1961, 3.

35. "Clarke Boys Complete Week at Forestry Camp," *Clarke County Democrat*, Aug. 24, 1961, 3.

36. "Ronald Padgett Attends Forestry Camp at Selma," *Clarke County Democrat*, Aug. 10, 1961, 3. The camp was held annually at Valley Creek State Park near Selma at "Camp Grist," a YMCA facility.

37. "Alabama Woodmen Meeting to Be Held in Birmingham Soon," *Union-Banner* (Clanton), Mar. 9, 1933, 2. In the lead-up to the 1931 "state-wide head camp meeting" to be held in Montgomery, it was noted W.O.W. owned "more than $800,000 worth of Alabama municipal, county and state securities" ("President W. A. Fraser to Speak at W.O.W. Meeting in Alabama," *Ashland Progress*, Feb. 5, 1931, 6).

38. "Shocco Springs—Alabama's Ideal Summer Resort," *Times* (Montgomery), May 21, 1925, 2. The following three quotations come from the same source.

39. "Shocco Springs, Alabama's Largest Religious Retreat, to Dedicate New Lodge in Honor of 91-Year-Old Leader," *Abbeville Herald*, Jan. 7, 1999, 3.

## Chapter 2

1. "Burgamot," *Courier* (Butler), Sept. 13, 1882, 1. Opinion signed "East Oaktuppa."

2. "Burgamot," *Courier* (Butler), Nov. 15, 1883, 6, by "Granger."

3. *Courier* (Butler), Oct. 18, 1883, 4.

4. "Notice," *Courier* (Butler), Oct. 11, 1883, 4.

5. "Protracted Meeting in Tuskaloosa," *Independent Monitor* (Tuscaloosa), Oct. 19, 1842, 2. The camp meeting's "manifestations of a serious and inquiring spirit in the community" resulted in a "protracted meeting at the Methodist church in this city" that appeared to have resulted in the forgiveness of sin of another "35 or 40," an estimate based on reports from the ministers and the numbers who occupied the "anxious seat." That was the seat or bench at a revival meeting reserved for those with a bad conscience, under conviction by the Holy Ghost, or in a state of anxiety over their spiritual condition.

6. "Oaktuppa Camp Meeting," by A TENTER, *Choctaw County News*, Oct. 1, 1879, 2.

7. "Camp Meeting," *Clarke County Democrat*, Oct. 23, 1879, 1.

8. "Choctaw County News," *Clarke County Democrat*, Oct. 6, 1881, 1.

9. "Choctaw County News," *Clarke County Democrat*, Oct. 20, 1881, 1.

10. *Choctaw Herald* (Butler), Sept. 24, 1885, 3.

11. "Great Revival Meeting," *Demopolis Times*, Sept. 7, 1916, 1.

12. "Butler News," *Choctaw County News* (Butler), Sept. 21, 1876, 3.

13. "Camp Meeting," *Clarke County Democrat*, Aug. 6, 1896, 4.

14. "Camp Meeting," *Selma Times*, Sept. 15, 1882, 4.

15. Bill Nye, "No More Frontier," *Clarke County Democrat*, June 19, 1884, 3.

16. *Choctaw Herald* (Butler), Sept. 24, 1885, 3.

17. *Clarke County Democrat*, Oct. 23, 1879, 1. That camp meeting appears to have been at Union Church, where Dr. Wadsworth and "the Rev. Mr. Morris of the Saint Stephens circuit, were the only ministers present from a distance." It was said the meeting was a good one, but "not very successful in the way of accessions to the church" (*Clarke County Democrat*, Oct. 2, 1879, 4).

18. "Letter from Tuskegee," *Opelika Times*, Aug. 22, 1884, 8. The following quotation is also from this source.

19. "Notice," *Clarke County Democrat*, May 27, 1915, 1.

20. That's the report the reverend was scheduled to give as a committee member when the South Bethel Association met on the first Sunday in Oct. 1887 at Lower Peach Tree, AL. (*Clarke County Democrat*, Sept. 15, 1887, 1.)

21. "Plain Facts," *Choctaw Advocate* (Butler), Aug. 2, 1922, 4.

22. "E. P. Chapman Answers Last Summons," *Clarke County Democrat*, Apr. 1, 1920, 1.

23. "Report of Fifth Sunday Meeting," *Clarke County Democrat*, Feb. 11, 1897, 1.

24. "The District Meeting," *Clarke County Democrat*, Oct. 13, 1887, 4.

25. "Program," *Clarke County Democrat*, Nov. 19, 1896, 1.

26. "Report of Fifth Sunday Meeting," 1.

27. "Centennial Meeting," *Clarke County Democrat*, July 7, 1892, 1.

28. Rev. H. B. Urquhart, "Camp Meeting Notes," *Elba Clipper*, July 26, 1910, 1.

29. Frank V'illis Barnett, "Dixons Mills Scene of Camp Meeting," *Birmingham News*, Jan. 31, 1932, 11. The quotations in the following two paragraphs come from the same source.

30. Urquhart, "Camp Meeting Notes," 1.

31. "Pea River Camp Meeting," *Elba Clipper*, July 22, 1910, 1.

32. "The Camp Meeting," *Clarke County Democrat*, May 29, 1879, 1.

33. "The Camp-Meeting," *Clarke County Democrat*, Sept. 18, 1879, 1.

34. "Letter from Tuskegee," 8.

35. Barnett, "Dixons Mills Scene of Camp Meeting," 11.

36. *Democrat-Reporter* (Linden), Sept. 30, 1926, 5.

37. "Marengo Camp Meeting," *Demopolis Times*, June 2, 1927, 2. The same article ran on the front page of the *Democrat-Reporter* in Linden on June 9.

38. "Marengo Camp Meeting," 2.

39. "Gypsy Pat Smith Drawing Crowds," *Montgomery Advertiser*, July 28, 1926, 10.

40. "Marengo Camp Meeting," 2.

41. "Leading Steps in Life of Gypsy Pat Smith," *Democrat-Reporter* (Linden), May 13, 1926, 1.

42. "Marengo Camp Meeting," 2. Pat Smith joined the Tyneside Scottish brigade of the Northumberland Fusiliers as a private ("Gypsy Pat Smith to Evangelize in U.S.," *Los Angeles Evening Herald*, Jan. 6, 1920, A-11).

43. "Gypsy Smith Again," *Marion County News*, Jan. 7, 1909, 3. The article noted that Rodney Gypsy Smith had already made four tours in the United States and had held religious meetings in New York, Boston, Philadelphia, Washington, and Denver among other cities and Pittsburg was making ready for his arrival.

44. "Gypsy Smith Will Speak on Monday," *Birmingham News*, Apr. 21, 1918, 7.

45. "Smith Revival Huge Success," *Montgomery Advertiser*, Aug. 3, 1926, 9. Referring to the Dixons Mill camp meeting, the article noted that the orchestra included three saxophones, three violins and a piano. Gypsy Pat Smith attributed his "faultless grammar" to "first, the Grace of God. . . . Second, assimilation. As I have lived and read I have unconsciously been educated; and third, the great gypsy latent quality of music. All Romanies are musical and anything ungrammatical grates on my ear" ("Leading Steps," 1).

46. "Gypsy Smith to Arrive Saturday for Tent Meeting," *Decatur Daily*, Mar 25, 1927, 1.

47. "Birmingham Won't Get Proposed Auditorium," *Montgomery Advertiser*, Sept. 5, 1911, 2.

48. "Auditorium Stock Company Formed," *Birmingham News*, July 10, 1913, 7.

49. "Evangelist Gypsy Smith Objects to Use [of] Name in Savannah Campaign," *Montgomery Times*, Dec. 11, 1922, 8.

50. C. C. Seay, "Bring Out Best in Nature, Plea of Gypsy Smith," *Selma Times Journal*, Nov. 21, 1929, 8.

51. "One Evangelist," *Russell Register* (Seale), Sept. 30, 1921, 2. The article appeared to have originated in the *Philadelphia Ledger*.

52. "Communicated," *Tuscaloosa News*, July 1, 1927, 4.

53. "The Wrong Gypsy," *Montgomery Advertiser*, July 3, 1927, 4.

54. "'Gypsy' Pat Smith Divorce Is Served," *Tuscaloosa News*, July 22, 1927, 1.

55. "'Gypsy' Smith's Creed Fails Him," *Hartford Courant* (CT), July 3, 1927, 37.

56. "Gypsy Smith Asks Divorce for Cruelty," *The Journal* (Meriden, CT), July 22, 1927, 9.

57. "Co-Respondent Is Named by Wife of 'Gypsy' Pat Smith," *Bridgeport Telegram* (CT), July 26, 1927, 1. Elsewhere that condition was described as a "permanent ailment which tenders intercourse dangerous" ("Gypsy Pat Smith and Wife Ready for Court Fight," *Bridgeport Telegram* [CT], Feb. 14, 1928, 11).

58. "Gypsy Smith Asks Divorce for Cruelty," *The Journal* (Meriden, CT), July 22, 1927, 9.

59. "Gypy [*sic*] Smith's Wife Is Granted Divorce," *The Journal* (Meriden, CT), June 22, 1928, 1. Also, under the following clumsy headline, "Darien Man Awarded Divorce from Gypsy Pat," in the *Record-Journal* (Meriden, CT), June 23, 1928, 15. Other reporting appeared, which indicated Gypsy Pat's property was foreclosed on by the bank and that he settled with a contractor

for nonpayment for labor and materials (*BridgeportTelegram* [CT], Mar. 16, 1928, 24; *Hartford Courant*, Apr. 12, 1928, 18).

60. "Gypsy Pat Smith and Wife Ready for Court Fight," 11. Concerning the societal repercussions of the divorce, Karin Tjader Smith was the daughter of the late Richard Tjader, a renowned explorer, big-game hunter, and sportsman. Her stepmother was a wealthy woman who had always surrounded herself with evangelists and missionaries as a result of her interest in religion. Capt. Gypsy Pat Smith had been one of Mrs. Tjader's protégés; he was a World War hero and famous for selling $2 million worth of Liberty Loans. Gypsy Pat was preaching in a Fifth Avenue church in New York when he met Miss Karin Tjader, when she was in her early twenties. They were eventually married in what was described as a "fashionable Fifth Avenue church" ("'Gypsy' Smith's Creed Fails Him," 37).

61. "Ten Thousand Hear 'Gypsy Pat' Speak," *Montgomery Advertiser*, Aug. 1, 1927, 10.

62. "'Gypsy' Seeks Divorce," *Birmingham News*, July 21, 1927, 1.

63. "Ten Thousand Hear 'Gypsy Pat' Speak," 10.

64. "Gypsy Pat Smith And Wife Ready For Court Fight," 11. Regarding Karin Smith traveling with her husband, in early 1926 it was "Gypsy Pat, Mrs. Smith and Gypsy Pat Jr." leaving Illinois for Tallahassee, Florida, for another evangelistic endeavor. In Illinois, it was said Gypsy Pat spoke to "overflowing crowds"—"hundreds were turned away"—in Marion and Harrisburg. The Gypsy Pat Smith family appeared in the First Methodist churches in the evangelist's speaking engagements.

65. It's worth noting that the *Daily Worker* in New York, the publication of the Communist Party USA, put the divorce in terms of destruction: "Evangelist's Home Wrecked" was the caption of a short notice referring to the "property dispute over the Smith residence" (July 22, 1927, 3).

66. *Selma Times-Journal*, Aug. 8, 1926, 11.

67. "Milestones," *Time*, July 2, 1928. On a personal note, the author believes that a photo that ran in the *Bridgeport Telegram* (CT) ("Gypsy Pat Smith and Wife Ready for Court Fight," 11), a photo that purported to be Gypsy Pat, was instead Rodney Gypsy Smith. If I am in error in that regard, I won't be as error stricken as *Time* reporting was in the matter in 1928.

68. "Letters," *Time*, July 16, 1928. The response to the letter was this: "TIME deeply regrets its error, proffers herewith apology to famed original Gypsy Smith, whose real name is Rodney Smith and who said: 'Jesus Christ was the greatest gentleman the world ever knew.'—ED."

69. "Great Crowds at Last Days of Marengo Meet," *Selma Times-Journal*, July 27, 1925, 3.

70. "Seventh-Day Adventists Hold Successful Meeting," *Union-Banner* (Clanton), Sept. 22, 1921, 3.

71. "Large Crowds Hear Noted Evangelist at Dixon's Mills," *Selma Times-Journal*, Aug. 6, 1927, 2. At least as early as 1921, "Capt. W. C. Blasingame of the U.S. Public Health Service" was pictured in an ad relative to the Marengo County Union Camp, "Ten Days of Recreation and Inspiration," in which it was noted the good doctor "has an important message to deliver on subjects of vital importance." See *Democrat-Reporter* (Linden), Aug. 4, 1921, 4.

72. "Fifth Sunday Meeting," *Elba Clipper*, July 26, 1910, 1.

73. "Camp Meeting and Training School to Be Held in July," *Montgomery Advertiser*, June 7, 1919, 3.

## Chapter 3

1. *Clarke County Democrat*, Sept. 27, 1883, 1.

2. "The Camp-Meeting," *Union Springs Herald*, Sept. 22, 1880, 3. The "dragoons of Claverhouse" and "Scotch covenanters" is a reference to king's soldiers interrupting a worship service in 1679 in Drumclog, Scotland.

3. "Our Correspondents—Our Auburn Items," *Opelika Times*, Aug. 31, 1877, 3.

4. William D. Parker, "History of Ozark and Dale County," *Southern Star* (Ozark), Oct. 26, 1939, 4. The serial article that appeared in the *Southern Star* was the Master of Science history thesis by W. D. Parker at Auburn University in 1933 ("Star to Publish History of Ozark and Dale County," Oct. 19, 1939, 1). Parker was identified at the time the serial ran as the "popular New York Life Insurance representative" in Ozark.

5. "The Swamp Secret—A Story of the Frontier" (Chapter XVIII), *North Alabamian*, (Tuscumbia), Jan. 19, 1900, 3.

6. *Clarke County Democrat*, Nov. 24, 1880, 1. The same publication reported in the Dec. 1, 1880, issue that the bill passed (1).

7. *Montgomery Advertiser*, Nov. 21, 1873, 2.

8. *Weekly Advertiser*, (Montgomery), Feb. 24, 1887, 3.

9. "Caption of Acts," *Weekly Advertiser* (Montgomery), Feb. 24, 1885, 7.

10. *Montgomery Advertiser*, Mar. 1, 1887, 2–3.

11. *Clarke County Democrat*, Oct. 23, 1884, 1.

12. *Opelika Times*, Aug. 19, 1876, 3.

13. *Union Springs Herald*, Sept. 7, 1881, 3.

14. "Pea River Camp Meeting," 1.

15. *Brewton Banner*, Oct. 15, 1885, 4. One of the "tents of distraction" was "Hotels," as tent-holders were encouraged to "make ample provision and provide accommodations for all who may come."

16. William George, letter, "Camp Meeting in Little Texas," *Opelika Times*, July 15, 1881, 3.

17. *Greenville Advocate*, July 6, 1882, 3.

18. "The Camp-Meeting," 3.

19. "The Camp Meeting at Unity Grove," *West Alabamian*, (Carrollton), Oct. 14, 1885, 3.

20. "Short Locals," *Troy Messenger*, Dec. 15, 1892, 5.

21. "The Little Texas Camp Meeting," *Montgomery Advertiser*, Aug. 21, 1884, 2. The reference was from a letter by EBENEZER to the editor entitled "Little Texas Camp Ground, Macon County, Aug. 17, 1884."

22. "Unity Grove Camp Meeting," *West Alabamian* (Carrollton), Oct. 21, 1885, 3.

23. "Butler News," 3.

24. "Oaktuppa Camp Meeting," 2.

25. "Greenville," *Montgomery Advertiser*, Oct. 13, 1886, 2. The reporting indicated that it hadn't rained in the area for two months and "the dust is almost unbearable."

26. "The Texasville Camp-Meeting," *Eufaula Daily Times*, Nov. 5, 1892, 1. Texasville is in Barbour County.

27. "Bob Jones Here," *Montgomery Advertiser*, Sept. 29, 1907, 25. As the Alabama-native hop-scotched across the state with his unyielding prohibition message to locations such as Pine Hill, Dothan, Evergreen, Elba, Greenville, and Camden, places such as Camden and Dothan "abolished the dispensary after his meetings."

28. "Great Crowds at Last Days of Marengo Meet," 3.

29. "The Camp-Meeting," 3.

30. *Choctaw County News* (Butler), Sept. 21, 1876, 3.

31. *Clarke County Democrat*, Aug. 16, 1883, 4.

32. *Clarke County Democrat*, Aug. 2, 1883, 4.

33. *Clarke County Democrat*, Aug. 23, 1883, 1.

34. *Times and News* (Eufaula), Aug. 4, 1885, 1. The newspaper incorrectly identified Asbury camp meeting as being in Marengo County.

35. "Big Camp-Meeting at Little Texas," 1.

36. "The Camp Meeting," 3.

37. "Culpepper Pranks," 4.

38. *Troy Messenger*, July 28, 1887, 5. Ramage Springs camp meeting was in Pike County.

39. *Choctaw Herald* (Butler), Sept. 25, 1902, 1. Frost's Bridge was near the Alabama line, east of Waynesboro, Miss.

40. Edmund Blair, "W-A-K-E of the N-E-W-S," *St. Clair News-Aegis*

(Pell City), Aug. 13, 1953, 1. Blair noted that while camp meetings were "fast dwindling away," one was yet held annually in the Pell City area, "on the camp grounds built by the Wesleyan Methodist church near Eden on highway 78."

41. Elder William Ashcraft, "Circular Letter," *Pickens County Herald and West Alabamian* (Carrollton), Nov. 20, 1867, 1.

42. "Butler News," 3. It's interesting to note that the editor apologized for that particular issue of the newspaper and placed the blame thusly: "We hope our readers will pardon the manner in which the outside pages of this issue are printed. We can not [*sic*] account for it, except by saying all hands were in a hurry to get off to Camp meeting."

43. "A Sad Case," *Montgomery Advertiser*, Sept. 19, 1885, 1.

44. "A Sad Case Denied," *Montgomery Advertiser*, Sept. 20, 1885, 2.

45. "Union Springs," *Montgomery Advertiser*, Sept. 23, 1885, 1.

46. *Southern Star* (Ozark), Sept. 30, 1885, 2.

47. "Local Intelligence," *Choctaw County News*, Aug. 21, 1879, 3.

48. "Smith Revival Huge Success," 9.

49. "Thomasville News," *Selma Times-Journal*, Aug. 7, 1927, 6.

50. "Local Affairs," *Union Springs Herald*, Sept. 25, 1889, 1.

51. "The First of the Kind," *Montgomery Advertiser*, Aug. 20, 1893, 6. It was noted that Professor Washington "is ever awoke to the interests of his race," and the Summer Assembly started out as an experiment "to provide recreation and instruction for tired colored ministers, teachers and other professional men and their families," but, due to its success, could become permanent at Tuskegee.

52. *Brewton Leader*, Oct. 3, 1893, 3.

53. "News Of Dora," *Daily Mountain Eagle* (Jasper), June 28, 1922, 6.

54. "Our Correspondents—Our Auburn Items," 3.

55. "Josh Billings," *Times and News* (Eufaula), Sept. 7, 1881, 3. The word not spelled out was spelled out in the article.

## Chapter 4

1. M. E. Billings, *Crimes of Preachers in the United States and Canada*, 10th ed. (New York: Truth Seeker Company). Downloaded as an ebook from Project Gutenberg e-book, released Aug. 24, 2018. The 10th edition compilation of ministers and their crimes said this on the title page: "Transcribed out of the Original Newspapers, and with Previous Transcriptions Diligently Compared and Revised." Also, the title page cited a couple of scriptural references: "These Be Thy Gods, O Israel" and "By their fruits shall ye know these. Do men gather grapes of thorns, or figs of thistles?"

2. *Columbia Recorder* (Columbia), Apr. 30, 1891, 4. When the story ap-

peared in the *Eufaula Daily Times*, Apr. 30, 1891, 3, it did so under the headline "Goodbye Silas."

3. A couple of the categories appeared in the book in author's quotation marks, as in "Conduct unbecoming a minister of the gospel" and "Fornication." Also, the difference between "Rape of girls under age of consent or puberty" (76 cases) and "Seduction of girls under fifteen" (28 cases) is confusing but must have made sense to the author. The denominations listed for most crimes were Methodist (728), Baptist (492), Catholic (325), Presbyterian (187), and Episcopalian (164), as well as others with lower numbers. My favorite clergy crimes listed included "Counterfeiting" (16), "Grave Robbery" (1), "Horse Stealing" (19), "Praying for death of neighbor, who died" (1), and crimes not designated as to number of cases, "dueling," "bankwrecking," "prize-fighting," "quackery," "coercion of the dying," "illicit manufacture of cigars," "slave-holding (by a missionary)," "jury fixing," "attempted train-wrecking," and "dynamiting."

4. "Public Speaking," *Choctaw County News* (Butler), Sept. 21, 1876, 3.

5. "Camp Meeting," an ad in the *Hartford Courant* (CT), Aug. 10, 1830, 3.

6. "Camp Meeting," *Pittsfield Sun* (Pittsfield, MA), Sept. 9, 1830, 3. The italics were in the original.

7. "Avery's Trial," *Boston Morning Post*, May 23, 1833, 1–2. It was noted that morning's coverage contained the government's evidence against Ephraim K. Avery, and, "Our report may not be perfect, yet we believe it contains all that is essential in the testimony." One could see that the *Boston Morning Post* knew the murder trial was a big story since it instructed readers how to get extra copies of the newspaper.

8. The *Democrat* (Huntsville) coverage of the Avery trial began on July 11, 1833, on the front page and continued through the month as the trial unfolded.

9. The reward for E. K. Avery's apprehension was $300. The reporting noted, "Mr. Avery asserts that he left Rhode Island only at the urgent solicitation of his legal advisers and friends, to avoid the fury and excitement of the people against him. He was visited last evening by a number of his professional brethren, and left the city, in company of the Sheriff, at 5 o,clock [*sic*] this morning, for Fall River."

10. *Fall River Daily Evening News* (MA), Mar. 23, 1866, 1.

11. "An Historic Murder Case," *Fall River Globe* (MA), Nov. 9, 1909, 8.

12. "Miscellany. The Case of Avery," *The Vermont Patriot and State Gazette* (Montpelier, VT), Mar. 25, 1833, 1.

13. "Avery's Trial," *Boston Morning Post*, 2.

14. "The Trial of E. K. Avery," *Democrat* (Huntsville), July 25, 1833, 1.

15. "Avery's Trial," *Pittsfield Sun*, May 30, 1833, 1.

16. "An Historic Murder Case," 8.

17. "Avery's Trial," *Boston Morning Post*, 1.

18. "Mr. Avery Acquitted," *Pittsfield Sun*, June 6, 1833, 3; June 13, 1833, 3.

19. "Report of a Committee of the New England Conference of the Methodist Episcopal Church, on the case of Rev. Ephraim Kingsbury Avery," *Boston Post*, June 14, 1833, 2. In the July 20, 1833, issue of the *Boston Post*, the newspaper cited "The Washington Globe" on page 2 noting an agent of the New England Methodist Conference was traveling across the country soliciting funds to pay for Reverend Avery's defense expenses. Two churches in Washington had contributed $150 to that end, total expenses said to be $6,000. The conference itself had contributed $1,000, but it was said "that several of their society had made themselves responsible for the whole sum."

20. "Trial of Rev. Isaac S. Kalloch," *The Liberator* (Boston, MA), Apr. 17, 1857, 3, citing the *Newburyport Herald*.

21. "Rev. E. K. Avery," *Boston Post*, Sept. 3, 1833, 2.

22. "Narration of the Apprehension, in Rindge, N.H., of the Rev. E. K. Avery, by Colonel Harvey Harnden, written by himself," *Boston Post*, Feb. 23, 1833, 2. "X," who critiqued the pamphlet, described it as "amusing and interesting" and abounding "in proofs of the courage, skill and shrewdness of the gallant author." The critique was biting to say the least, pointing out that while Harnden, a soldier of some fame, unfortunately did not add to his legend by arresting Avery without firing a shot, he was fortunate in parlaying his secret mission to catch and arrest the infamous preacher into cash and horses and the like by sharing his secret with others along the way. Also, on the forty-third anniversary of the great Fall River fire of July 2, 1843, an accounting was made of property destroyed during the blaze. Among the more than six hundred names mentioned in the thirty-four-page pamphlet was "Harvey Harnden, the officer who captured the famous Rev. E. K. Avery, the alleged murderer of Maria Cornell, and for many years a successful auctioneer, met with a loss of $1,105" ("A Remembrance of the Fire," *Fall River Daily Herald* (MA), July 3, 1886, 4).

23. *The Liberator* (Boston, MA), Jan. 25, 1834, 4. The source for the pamphlet was "The Zion's Herald (Methodist)." When the pamphlet was made available to the public, it included a statement of facts from the Reverend Avery concerning how he became involved in the prosecution of Sarah Cornell's death and "a map" (*Boston Post*, Feb. 13, 1834, 3).

24. "Old South," *Fall River Monitor* (MA), May 30, 1835, 2.

25. *New England Farmer* (Boston, MA), May 16, 1857, 3.

26. "Richmond," *Berkshire County Eagle* (Pittsfield, MA), Mar. 12 and Mar. 19, 1868, 2.

27. "Enjoys Spoken and Silent Drama," *Evening Herald* (Fall River, MA), Dec. 15, 1919, 8.

28. *Indianapolis Star*, Jan. 19, 1930, 12.

29. "Communications—Abolition and Universalism," by "A Universalist Abolitionist," *The Liberator* (Boston, MA), Jan. 25, 1839, 2.

30. "E. K. Avery," *Fall River Monitor* (MA), Mar. 21, 1835, 2, citing "The Springfield Pioneer, Ohio."

31. *Jacksonville Republican*, Feb. 24, 1866, 4. See also *Alabama Beacon* (Greensboro), Feb. 16, 1866, 1. Another version of the story identified the clergyman as "a Methodist minister," and his vision involved two angels announcing E. K. Avery's innocence (*Fall River Daily Evening News* (MA), Apr. 2, 1908, 10).

32. "Taught A Forcible Lesson In Advertising," *Eufaula Daily Times*, Apr. 11, 1891, 1.

33. *Evening Herald* in Fall River, MA, published the story ("Barnum as Rev. E. K. Avery") in its Jan. 24, 1911, issue (9). The story was cited as appearing in Barnum's "Autobiography," and Barnum said he heard such shouts from the mob who thought he was Avery as "the lecherous old hypocrite," "the sanctimonious murderer," "the black-coated villain," "lynch the scoundrel," "let's tar and feather him," "you needn't roll your sanctimonious eyes," "remember the stockyard," and "we'll show him how to hang poor factory girls." The point of the lesson, according to Turner: "My dear Barnum . . . you will see that this will be noised about town as a trick played by one of the circus managers upon the other, and our pavilion will be crammed tomorrow night." Barnum said, "It was even so," but also that it was a long time before he forgave Turner for the joke.

34. "Items of News," *Daily Selma Reporter*, Sept. 5, 1835, 2.

35. "Another Strange Story," *York Gazette* (PA), Jan. 16, 1844, 2.

36. "Rev. E. K. Avery," *Tri-Weekly Nashville Union* (TN), Jan. 23, 1844, 3.

37. *Flag of the Union* (Tuscaloosa), Aug. 4, 1841, 3.

38. "Rev. E. K. Avery," *Fall River Daily Evening News* (MA), Mar. 23, 1866, 1.

39. "Report of a Committee of the New England Conference," 2.

40. "Not Camp Meeting," *Montgomery Advertiser*, Feb. 15, 1885, 1.

41. "Teaching Before Learning," *Clarke County Democrat*, Aug. 5, 1880, 3.

42. *Clarke County Democrat*, Oct. 17, 1895, 1.

43. "Took Unnecessary Risk," *Hamilton News-Press* (Hamilton), Oct. 24, 1895, 2.

## Chapter 5

1. "Murder in Cane Creek!" *Clarke County Democrat*, Dec. 27, 1888, 4. The *Birmingham News* identified Sam Walker as "a prominent white farmer of Clay county" ("Three for Life," Nov. 16, 1889, 6).

2. "Local News," *Clarke County Democrat*, Dec. 19, 1889, 4.

3. "The Hanging of Fed Kidd," *Clarke County Democrat*, Jan. 9, 1890, 4. "Sheriff Chapman, assisted by his deputy, W. J. Taylor, attended to all the details of the sad event, and everything passed off quietly and in order. We were glad to see so few persons in town that day. The hanging took place within the jail wall, and the spectators were in number and character as provided by law. This is the third legal hanging that has occurred in the county within the last thirty-five or forty years, and may many more years pass away before there is a necessity for another."

4. "Fred Kidd Hung," *Weekly Advertiser* (Montgomery), Jan. 9, 1890, 2. The article noted three others sentenced with Fred Kidd in the killing were sentenced to life in prison. The *Birmingham News* under "Three for Life" cited in note 1 said this: "This morning Deputy P. J. Rogers of the Tennessee Coal, Iron and Railroad Company at Pratt Mines, brought in five negro convicts from Grove Hill, Clarke county, and carried them out to the mines to serve their sentences." Three of the five were those sentenced in the killing of Sam Walker, their names appearing in the account as "Alex Kidd, Charles Legett and Will Murreth."

5. "Events of the Past—Happenings of Interest as Chronicled by Democrat of November 14, 1889," *Clarke County Democrat*, Dec. 23, 1920, 1.

6. From a single sheet of paper in my possession and attributed this way: Rev. T. H. Ball, A.M.[,], entry entitled "J. H. Fendley," *A Glance into the Great South-East, or Clarke County, Alabama and Its Surroundings, from 1540 to 1877* (Tuscaloosa: Willo Publishing Company, 1879), page number not cited. Another single sheet of paper in my possession was from 1923 and John Simpson Graham's *History of Clarke County* (Birmingham, Birmingham Printing Company), page number not cited, said, among other things, that "J. H. Fendley" was "said to have baptized and married more people than any one in Clarke County."

7. "Fatted Calf," *Weekly Advertiser* (Montgomery), Dec. 1, 1887, 9; "A Colored Prodigal Son," *Memphis Avalanche*, Nov. 14, 1887, 2. The *Jacksonville Republican*, Oct. 7, 1887, 2, made note that the fatted calf ended up feeding "nearly two thousand colored people" at the camp meeting.

8. "A Colored Camp Meeting," *Pantagraph* (Bloomington, IL), Sept. 16, 1887, 4.

9. *Salem Herald-Advocate* (IL), Oct. 7, 1887, 2.

10. "Interesting Discussion on Camp Meetings," *Selma Times*, May 16, 1884, 4.

11. Actually, apart from the camp-meeting issue, the ecclesiastical life of the races followed a parallel course. According to an article in the *Selma*

*Times*, one Rev. J. B. Stansberry at the conference appealed a case of immorality against the Rev. C. H. Green, who had been suspended by the New Jersey Annual Conference for the charge, unspecified in the reporting. "Stansberry" was in all likelihood the Rev. John B. Stansbury, who appeared at the Baltimore conference fresh from the church wars in Connecticut. A church split, a phenomenon that white Protestant churches were all too familiar with, along with clergy immorality, had consumed Stansbury starting in late 1883. It seems he was appointed by the Bishop of the A.M.E. Church to fill the pulpit at Bethel A.M.E. Church in New Haven, Connecticut. The church, which had wearied of the bishop's delay in appointing a minister, went out and found one of its own. When Stansbury appeared, several members of the church leadership marched in one Sunday morning in mid-sermon and forcibly removed him from the pulpit. Stansbury ended up holding services with a minority of Bethel members in the Masonic hall in the city, while the church brought back the previous minister. The three men who removed Stansbury from the pulpit were arrested. The church matter went to city court, where Stansbury accused the men of assault. The "Bethel colored church trouble," as it was deemed, ended up in the court record along with alleged crimes like an axe assault, attempted wife killings, attempted murder, arson, and various thefts ("The Court Record," *Daily Morning Journal and Courier* [New Haven, CT], Apr. 3, 1884, 2). Cf. "Colored Methodists" (Jan. 7, 1884, 2); "The Bethel Church Trouble" (Jan. 9, 1884, 2).

12. "Local Affairs," 1.

13. "The Nine Days' Wonder," *Greenville Advocate*, Feb. 21, 1883, 3.

14. *Greenville Advocate*, July 6, 1882, 3.

15. *Greenville Advocate*, Sept. 1, 1881, 3.

16. *Alabama Beacon* (Greensboro), Aug. 28, 1888, 4.

17. "City and County," *Selma Times*, Sept. 20, 1882, 4.

18. "Judy Brown Says (Strolling Around)," *Birmingham News*, Feb. 24, 1925, 21. Note these two references in the *Piedmont Inquirer* on page 1 of its July 9, 1892, issue. One: "Baseball. Coons. Piedmont and Tecumseh. The glorious 4th. Seven innings and a row. The end." Two: "When a man says he is going blackberrying it doesn't mean that he expects to attend a colored funeral."

19. *Courier* (Butler), June 28, 1882, 4.

20. *Alabama Courier* (Athens), June 22, 1882, 2.

21. "The Theatres," *Montgomery Advertiser*, Sept. 27, 1896, 9. The reference was to Al Field's minstrel show, praised repeatedly in the state and elsewhere for its family-oriented entertainment.

22. "Gener Lee Teal on Trial for Murder of Rev. Ed Brown," *Clayton Record*, Oct. 29, 1937, 1.

23. "Teal Given Life Sentence for Brown Murder," *Clayton Record*, Nov. 5, 1937, 1. One doctor at trial described Teal as having the intelligence of a child about "10 to 13 years and gave evidence of being a degenerate type, underdeveloped rather than insane."

24. "Teel Confesses to Sheriff He Aided in Murder of Brown," *Clayton Record*, July 30, 1937, 1.

25. "Gener Lee Teal On Trial," 1.

26. "Stevens Was Convicted," *Weekly Advertiser* (Montgomery), Aug. 28, 1903, 8.

27. "Hanging in Wedowee," *Weekly Advertiser* (Montgomery), Oct. 2, 1903, 10.

28. "Randolph's First Hanging," *Birmingham News*, Feb. 23, 1903, 2.

29. "Editorial Tidbits," *Roanoke Leader*, Apr. 29, 1903, 2.

30. "Tom Barsh," *Elba Clipper*, May 21, 1903, 7.

31. *Montgomery Advertiser*, May 1, 1903, 4.

32. "Stevens Was Convicted," 8.

33. "Sheriff Kent and His Duty," *Roanoke Leader*, Sept. 9, 1903, 2.

34. "The Star Rejoins," *Roanoke Leader*, Sept. 16, 1903, 2. The *Leader*, referring to the *Star*'s editorial page which read, "The Randolph Star Publishing Company Editor and Proprietor," noted it was generally known that the sheriff was the proprietor.

35. "The Star Rejoins," 3.

36. "The War Is Over," *Roanoke Leader*, Sept. 23, 1903, 2.

37. "Hanging at Widowee," *Birmingham News*, Oct. 9, 1903, 7. By comparison with Sharman Stevens, note a pardon granted by the governor of Alabama to a Black man a month or so before the Stevens hanging. John Brown of Limestone County "tried to reprove another negro who had been cursing near a respectable family when the two became involved in a difficulty." In the city of Athens, Alabama, Brown struck the other man with a piece of pine wood that caused the death of the man. Brown was sentenced to ten years in Oct. 1901, but now, two years later, was pardoned based on his intervention in behalf of the "respectable family" and, as the governor put it, "[Brown] had been an excellent negro and well liked by all with whom he came in contact."

38. *Courier* (Butler), Oct. 14, 1882, 3. Those were what "the girl of the period takes with her to camp-meeting."

39. "Local Matters," *Choctaw County News* (Butler), Sept. 21, 1876, 3. A reference to gastrointestinal problems.

40. A letter of Sept. 4, 1882, to Alabama Gov. R. W. Cobb signed by Choctaw County officials in response to a charge of lynching by a county mob. The letter was one of many "papers" regarding justification of the

lynching by county officials that appeared in the *Montgomery Advertiser* on Sept. 14, 1882, 2, under "The Choctaw Trouble."

41. "The Choctaw County Outragers," *Weekly Advertiser*, Oct. 7, 1874, 2.

42. *Selma Morning Times*, Apr. 14, 1870, 3. The *Times* described the editor from neighboring Wilcox County as a "genial, social gentleman, was a gallant soldier on the Confederate side in the late war, and . . . does not feel disposed to repent of his efforts to secure the independence of his native South." Indeed, the *Times* was of the opinion that Editor Col. Scott was a "better 'rebel' now" than when he enlisted in 1861; one who "never will forgive, or consent to forget, the damning wrongs which a Congressional oligarchy has inflicted upon his race and section."

43. "Negro Riot in Choctaw," *Clarke County Democrat*, Aug. 25, 1874, 1. Reporting by the Grove Hill paper was based on the "Mobile Register."

44. "Another Radical Lie," *Choctaw Herald* (Butler), Aug. 26, 1874, 2.

45. "How Radical Lies Are Manufactured," *Montgomery Advertiser*, Aug. 27, 1874, 2.

46. According to the *Advertiser*, the only way to counter the commission of outrages was to disappoint the Republicans. The way to do that, when possible, was to respond to the "'demonstrating' blacks in a spirit of kindness, show them how they have been deceived and betrayed, and get them to tell who put such folly in their heads."

47. "Exit Hays et id Omne," *Montgomery Advertiser*, Oct. 23, 1874, 2. The Latin meaning was loosely "Exit Hays and all of that kind."

48. "The Temper of the South," *Hartford Daily Courant*, Sept. 15, 1874, 1.

49. "The Hays-Hawley letter later was found to contain several overblown and even outright false accusations. Nevertheless, it did point to the tactics of violence and intimidation used by militant Democrats" (Matthew C. O'Neal, Auburn University, "Charles Hays," *Encyclopedia of Alabama*). Among others who made the Montgomery newspaper's need-to-exit list with Charles Hays was Alexander McKinstry, a former Confederate who became lieutenant governor and used parliamentary procedure to keep Democrats from controlling the state senate; P. W. K. Stringfellow, a former Confederate and Republican leader from Hale County; and Black US Congressmen J. T. Rapier and Jeremiah Haralson.

50. *Montgomery Advertiser*, Sept. 18, 1868, 4.

51. "Reconstruction acknowledged a Failure by the Radical Party in Alabama," *Jacksonville Republican*, Oct. 2, 1868, 2.

52. "General Correspondence," *Southern Republican* (Demopolis), Dec. 28, 1870, 4.

53. *Marengo News* (Demopolis), Sept. 5, 1874, 3.

54. "Address of the Democratic and Conservative State Executive Committee," *Choctaw Herald* (Butler), Oct. 14, 1874, 1.

55. "The Choctaw Trouble," *Montgomery Advertiser*, 2.

56. "The Choctaw Trouble," *Montgomery Advertiser*, 2.

57. "The Hanging in Choctaw," *Courier* (Butler), Sept. 6, 1882, 1.

58. "The Hanging in Choctaw," 3.

59. "Burgamot," *Courier* (Butler), Sept. 13, 1882, 1. Just days after the hanging, the *Courier* noted that the camp meeting at Smith's Camp Ground in Desotoville had been "indefinitely postponed" ("Local Items," Aug. 23, 2).

60. "Jack Turner Pays His Last Debt," *Livingston Journal*, Sept. 1, 1882, 2. The *Journal* called the alleged insurrection "a most hellish crime against humanity and civilization."

61. "Uprising of Negroes Checked—One Negro Hung," and "Insurrection in Choctaw County Nipped in Nick of Time" (letter to the editor of the *Montgomery Advertiser* from "G" in Butler, Ala., dated Aug. 19, 1882), *Opelika Times*, Aug. 25, 1882, 2.

62. "Choctaw County, Alabama—Grand Nego [*sic*] Conspiracy to Massacre the Whites, 'From the Cradle to the Grave,'" *Courier* (Butler), Sept. 6, 1882, 1.

63. "Gen. Jack Turner," *Troy Messenger*, Aug. 31, 1882, 4.

64. "The Plot Spread to Conecuh," *Montgomery Advertiser*, Sept. 12, 1882, 2.

65. *Courier* (Butler), Sept. 13, 1882, 1.

66. "Camden," *Montgomery Advertiser*, Aug. 1, 1888, 1.

67. "The Rifles' Picnic," *Wilcox Progressive Era* (Camden), May 8, 1889, 3.

68. "Soldiers Dinner," *Wilcox Progressive Era* (Camden), Jan. 16, 1889, 3.

69. *Wilcox Progressive Era* (Camden), Aug. 6, 1896, 3. The ladies wanted to know everything about the Wilcox Mounted Rifles who left Camden on Apr. 24, 1861; they wanted every scintilla of information on the Wilcox True Blues who left East Wilcox for Pensacola on Feb. 13, 1861.

70. "The Pine Hill Barbecue," *Wilcox Progressive Era* (Camden), Aug. 19, 1909, 3.

71. *Wilcox Progressive Era* (Camden), July 8, 1896, 2.

72. "Letter from Dundee," *Selma Morning Times*, May 9, 1871, 3.

73. "The Choctaw Trouble," *Morning Times* (Selma), Sept. 17, 1882, 3. The *Morning Times* list was taken from the list that appeared in Butler's *Courier* on Sept. 6, 1882, with minor changes in the charges, such as living in adultery, called "Adultery and Fornication" in the *Courier*.

74. "The Choctaw Conspiracy," *Opelika Times*, Aug. 25, 1882, 2.

75. "Correspondence Between Gov. Cobb and the County Officials," *Courier* (Butler), Oct. 21, 1882, 1.

76. This "Notice" appeared in the *Courier* on June 28, 1882, 4: "The Greenbackers of Choctaw County, Ala., will hold a meeting on Saturday next, the first day of July 1882, at Choctaw Camp Ground, for the purpose of nominating a candidate for Representative to the State Legislature. It is hoped that all the Beats will be fully represented."

77. *Courier* (Butler, AL), Sept. 6, 1882, 1. The article was from the *Eutaw Whig and Observer.*

78. "The Champion Liar of Alabama Interviewed by the New York Times on the Choctaw County Hanging," *Courier* (Butler), Sept. 6, 1882, 1. The last two quotations in this paragraph are also from this source.

79. "The Plotters Entrapped," *Livingston Journal*, Aug. 21, 1874, 2. The *Journal* reporting on the Billings murder is textbook for the time. The whipping boy, as usual, was the *State Journal* for its allegations that the KKK and/or Democrats were responsible for bushwhacking the man and his horse (also killed) in a hail of buckshot and bullets. Everybody, including the thirty-ish dead man, was painted with suspicious and questionable tones in the *Journal* account: Billings's business partner and a drunken associate; Blacks he associated with; even the wife, Juliette Billings, for writing to a friend, "I want to leave this dreadful country" and mentioning that she and her husband had been looking at a "fair crop" when he was killed. The *Journal* contacted a well-known planter in the area and had him check out the "fair crop" assessment made by the widow. The conclusion by the meddling neighbor was that much of the land was unworked or "badly worked," and the garden was mostly "weeds and grass."

80. "The Champion Liar of Alabama."

81. *Birmingham Age-Herald*, Aug. 24, 1897, 2. The dateline was Montgomery, and the story was "A special to the [Montgomery] Advertiser from Gadsden, Ala."

### Conclusion

1. "Bright Sparks from the [indecipherable word] Pen of Fair Mignonette," *Wilcox Progressive Era* (Camden), July 25, 1888, 2.

2. "Aunt Tab's Letter," *Wilcox Progressive Era* (Camden), June 27, 1888, 2. See also "Which Weilds [*sic*] the Greater Influence, Wealth or Education?" *Wilcox Progressive Era* (Camden), May 23, 1888, 2; "Should the Education of Woman Equal That of Man?" *Wilcox Progressive Era* (Camden), Aug. 1, 1888, 3; "Was Brutus Justifiable in the Assassination of Caesar?" *Wilcox Progressive Era* (Camden), Sept. 12, 1888, 2.

3. "Mignonette's Warblings," *Wilcox Progressive Era* (Camden), Sept. 12, 1888, 2.

4. "Our Circle," *Wilcox Progressive Era* (Camden), Apr. 10, 1889, 2. All of the quotations in the paragraph are from this source.

5. "Editor Wilcox Progress," *Wilcox Progressive Era* (Camden), May 23, 1888, 2.

6. "Aunt Tab's Letter," 2.

7. "Rev. J. H. Fendley Dies in Selma," *Clarke County Democrat*, Mar. 24, 1927, 1.

# Bibliography


### Books

Ball, T. H. *A Glance into the Great South-East, or Clarke County, Alabama and Its Surroundings, From 1540 to 1877.* (Tuscaloosa: Willo Publishing Company, 1879).

Billings, M. E. *Crimes of Preachers in the United States and Canada*, 10th ed. (New York: The Truth Seeker Company, n.d.). Released as a Project Gutenberg e-book on Aug. 24, 2018.

Graham, John Simpson. *History of Clarke County* (Birmingham: Birmingham Publishing Company, 1923).

### Newspapers

Author's note: Most of my sources were newspapers. Unless otherwise noted, these newspapers were published in many locations in Alabama.

*Abbeville Herald*

"Shocco Springs, Alabama's largest religious retreat, to dedicate new lodge in honor of 91-year-old leader." Jan. 7, 1999.

*Alabama Beacon* (Greensboro)

Feb. 16, 1866.

Aug. 28, 1888.

*Alabama Courier* (Athens)

June 22, 1882.

*Ashland Progress*

"President W. A. Fraser to Speak at W.O.W. Meeting in Alabama." Feb. 5, 1931.

*Berkshire County Eagle* (Pittsfield, MA)

"Richmond." Mar. 12 and 19, 1868.

*Birmingham Age-Herald*
"Race War Imminent." Aug. 24, 1897.

*Birmingham News*
"Auditorium Stock Company Formed." July 10, 1913.
Barnett, Frank V'illis. "Dixons Mills [*sic*] Scene of Camp Meeting." Jan. 31, 1932.
Greeley, Alfred W. "Freak Cults Under Name of Religion." Feb. 23, 1907.
"'Gypsy' Seeks Divorce." July 21, 1927.
"Gypsy Smith Will Speak on Monday." Apr. 21, 1918.
"Hanging at Widowee." Oct. 9, 1903.
"Judy Brown Says." Feb. 24, 1925.
"Randolph's First Hanging." Feb. 23, 1903.
"Three for Life." Nov. 16, 1889.

*Blue-Grass Blade* (Lexington, KY)
"Cane Ridge." Oct. 25, 1903.

*Boston Post*
"Avery's Trial." May 23, 1833.
Harnden, Colonel Harvey. "Narration of the Apprehension, in Rindge, N.H., of the Rev. E. K. Avery, by Colonel Harvey Harnden, written by himself." Feb. 23, 1833.
"Report of a Committee of the New England Conference of the Methodist Episcopal Church, or the Case of Rev. Ephraim Kingsbury Avery." June 14, 1833.
"Rev. E. K. Avery." Sept. 3, 1833.

*Brewton Banner*
"Camp Meeting." July 7, 1883.
Oct. 15, 1885.

*Brewton Leader*
Oct. 3, 1893.

*Brewton Standard*
"Camp Meetings." *New York Times Sunday Magazine*. Nov. 17, 1932.

*Bridgeport Telegram* (Bridgeport, CT)
"Co-Respondent Is Named by Wife of 'Gypsy' Pat Smith." July 26, 1927.
"Gypsy Pat Smith and Wife Ready for Court Fight." Feb. 14, 1928.
Mar. 16, 1928.

*Brownsville Herald* (Brownsville, TX)
"'Brute' Man Is Shut Out." Dec. 5, 1906.

*Central New Jersey Home News*
"New York Town Talk." Jan. 22, 1907.

*Centreville Press*
Rexford, Eben E. "The Swamp Secret—A Story of the Frontier (Chapters XIX & XX)." June 18, 1900.

*Chicago Tribune*
"Gluck Colonists Are Like Shadows." Aug. 28, 1907.

*Choctaw Advocate* (Butler)
"Plain Facts." Aug. 2, 1922.

*Choctaw County News* (Butler)
"Butler News." Sept. 21, 1876.
"Local Intelligence." Aug. 21, 1879.
"Local Matters." Sept. 21, 1876.
"Public Speaking." Sept. 21, 1876.
TENTER, A. "Oaktuppa Camp Meeting." Oct. 1, 1879.

*Choctaw Herald* (Butler)
"Address of the Democratic and Conservative State Executive Committee." Oct. 14, 1874.
"Another Radical Lie." Aug. 26, 1874.
Sept. 24, 1885.
Sept. 25, 1902.

*Clarke County Democrat* (Grove Hill)
"Agent Outlines Work of Conservation Corps." May 13, 1937.
Aug. 2, 1883.
Aug. 16, 1883.
Aug. 23, 1883.
"The Camp Meeting." May 29, 1879.
"Camp Meeting." Aug. 6, 1896.
"The Camp Meeting." Sept. 18, 1879.
"Camp Meeting." Oct. 23, 1879.
"Centennial Meeting." July 7, 1892.
"Choctaw County News." Oct. 6, 1881.
"Choctaw County News." Oct. 20, 1881.
"Clarke Boys Complete Work at Forestry Camp." Aug. 24, 1961.
"Clarke County Baptists Plan Boy's Camp Soon." July 28, 1955.
"Community Center Is Nearing Completion." July 25, 1940.
"The District Meeting." Oct. 13, 1887.

"E. P. Chapman Answers Last Summons." April 1, 1920.
"Events of the Past—Happenings of Interest as Chronicled by Democrat of November 14, 1889." Dec. 23, 1990.
"4-H Girls to Camp at Suggsville." June 30, 1949.
"The Hanging of Fed Kidd." Jan. 9, 1890.
"Local News." Dec. 19, 1889.
"Many Attend Opening of Camp Nickelojo." July 14, 1927.
"Murder In Cane Creek!" Dec. 27, 1888.
"Negro Riot in Choctaw." Aug. 25, 1874.
"Notice." May 27, 1915.
Nov. 24, 1880.
Nye, Bill. "No More Frontier." June 19, 1884.
Oct. 2, 1879.
Oct. 17, 1895.
Oct. 23, 1879.
Oct. 23, 1884.
"Program." Nov. 19, 1896.
"Report of Fifth Sunday Meeting." Feb. 11, 1897.
"Rev. J. H. Fendley Dies in Selma." Mar. 24, 1927.
"Rev. Paul Smith to Speak at Youth Retreat." Aug. 24, 1961.
"Ronald Padgett Attends Forestry Camp at Selma." Aug. 10, 1961.
Sept. 15, 1887.
Sept. 27, 1883.
"SONGS, ONE CENT EACH." Mar. 16, 1882.
"Sunbeam Day Camp at Camp Morvin." Aug. 10, 1961.
"Teaching Before Learning." Aug. 5, 1880.

*Clayton Record*
"Gener Lee Teal on Trial for Murder of Rev. Ed Brown." Oct. 29, 1937.
"Teal Given Life Sentence for Brown Murder." Nov. 5, 1937.
"Teel [*sic*] Confesses to Sheriff He Aided in Murder of Brown." July 30, 1937.

*Columbia Recorder*
Apr. 30, 1891.

*Courier* (Butler)
"Burgamot." Sept. 13, 1882.
"Burgamot." Nov. 15, 1883.
"The Champion Liar of Alabama Interviewed by the New York Times on the Choctaw County Hanging." Sept. 6, 1882.
"Choctaw County, Alabama—Grand Nego [*sic*] Conspiracy to Massacre the Whites, 'From Cradle to the Grave.'" Sept. 6, 1882.

"Correspondence Between Gov. Cobb and the County Officials." Oct. 21, 1882.
"The Hanging in Choctaw." Sept. 6, 1882.
June 28, 1882.
"Local Items." Aug. 23, 1882.
"Notice." June 28, 1882.
"Notice." Oct. 11, 1883.
Oct. 14, 1882.
Oct. 18, 1883.

*Courier-Journal* (Louisville, KY)
"Old Cane Ridge." Sept. 13, 1903.
Purvis, W. H. "A Kentucky Revival Meeting" (in *American Magazine*). Sept. 25, 1887.

*Daily Morning Journal and Courier* (New Haven, CT)
"The Bethel Church Trouble." Jan. 9, 1884.
"Colored Methodists." Jan. 7, 1884.
"The Court Record." Apr. 3, 1884.

*Daily Mountain Eagle* (Jasper)
"News of Dora." June 28, 1922.

*Daily Selma Reporter*
"Items of News." Sept. 5, 1835.

*Daily Worker* (New York)
July 22, 1927.

*Decatur Daily*
"Gypsy Smith To Arrive Saturday for Tent Meeting." Mar. 25, 1927.

*Democrat* (Huntsville)
"Trial of E. K. Avery." July 11, 1833.

*Democrat-Reporter* (Linden)
"J. M. Barkley Killed Monday Night." July 1, 1926
"Leading Steps in Life of Gypsy Pat Smith." May 13, 1926.
"Letter to Club Members." July 1, 1926.
Sept. 30, 1926.
"Ten Days of Recreation and Inspiration." Aug. 4, 1921.

*Demopolis Times*
"Great Revival Meeting." Sept. 7, 1916.
"Marengo Camp Meeting." June 2, 1927.

*Elba Clipper*
"Fifth Sunday Meeting." July 26, 1910.
"Pea River Camp Meeting." July 22, 1910.
"Tom Barsh." May 21, 1903.
Urquhart, Rev. H. B. "Camp Meeting Notes." July 26, 1910.

*Eufaula Daily Times*
"Goodbye Silas." Apr. 30, 1891.
"Taught a Forcible Lesson in Advertising." Apr. 11, 1891.+ Texasville Camp-Meeting." Nov. 5, 1892.

*Evening Herald* (Fall River, MA)
"Barnum as Rev. E. K. Avery." Jan. 24, 1911.
"Enjoys Spoken and Silent Drama." Dec. 15, 1919.

*Fall River Daily Evening News* (MA)
April 2, 1908.
"Rev. E. K. Avery." Mar. 23, 1866.

*Fall River Daily Herald* (MA)
"A Remembrance of the Fire." July 3, 1886.

*Fall River Globe* (MA)
"An Historic Murder Case." Nov. 9, 1909.

*Fall River Monitor* (MA)
"E. K. Avery." Mar. 21, 1835.
"Old South." May 30, 1835.

*Flag of Union* (Tuscaloosa)
Aug. 4, 1841.

*Greenville Advocate*
July 6, 1882.
"The Nine Days' Wonder." Feb. 21, 1883.
Sept. 1, 1881.

*Hamilton News-Press*
"Took Unnecessary Risk." Oct. 24, 1895.

*Hartford Courant* (CT)
Apr. 12, 1928.
"Camp Meeting" (ad). Apr. 10, 1830.
"'Gypsy' Smith's Creed Fails Him." July 3, 1927.
"The Temper of the South." Sept. 15, 1874.

*Houston Post* (TX)
"Adamless Eden." Dec. 20, 1906.

*Independent Monitor* (Tuscaloosa)
"Protracted Meeting in Tuskaloosa." Oct. 19, 1842.

*Indianapolis Star*
Jan. 19, 1930.

*Jacksonville Republican*
Feb. 24, 1866.
Oct. 7, 1887.
"Reconstruction acknowledged a Failure by the Radical Party in Alabama." Oct. 2, 1868.

*Journal* (Meriden, CT)
"Gypsy Smith Asks Divorce for Cruelty." July 22, 1927.
"Gypy [*sic*] Smith's Wife Is Granted Divorce." June 22, 1928.

*Lexington Herald* (Lexington, KY)
"Birth of Christian Church at Historic 'Cane Ridge Meeting House' Is Recalled in Memorial Services for James Rogers." May 29, 1921.

*Liberator* (Boston, MA)
"Abolitionist, a Universal." "Communications—Abolition and Universalism." Jan. 25, 1839.
Jan. 25, 1834.
"Trial of Rev. Isaac S. Kalloch." Apr. 17, 1857.

*Livingston Journal*
"Jack Turner Pays His Last Debt." Sept. 1, 1882.
"The Plotters Entrapped." Aug. 21, 1874.

*Los Angeles Evening Herald*
"Gypsy Pat Smith to Evangelize in U.S." Jan. 6, 1920.

*Marengo News* (Demopolis)
Sept. 5, 1874.

*Marion County News*
"Gypsy Smith Again." Jan. 7, 1909.

*Memphis Avalanche*
"A Colored Prodigal Son." Nov. 14, 1887.

*Montgomery Advertiser*
"Birmingham Won't Get Proposed Auditorium." Sept. 5, 1911.

"Bob Jones Here." Sept. 29, 1907.
"Camden." Aug. 1, 1888.
"Camp Meeting And Training School To Be Held In July." June 7, 1919.
"The Choctaw Trouble." Sept. 14, 1882.
"Culpepper Pranks." May 30, 1904.
"Ebenezer." "Little Texas Camp Ground, Macon County, Aug. 17, 1884." Aug. 21, 1884.
"Exit Hays et id Omne." Oct. 23, 1874.
"The First Of The Kind." Aug. 20, 1893.
"Greenville." Oct. 13, 1886.
"Gypsy Pat Smith Drawing Crowds." July 28, 1926.
"How Radical Lies Are Manufactured." Aug. 27, 1874.
"The Little Texas Camp Meeting." Aug. 21, 1884.
March 1, 1887.
May 1, 1903.
"Not Camp Meeting." Feb. 15, 1885.
Nov. 21, 1873.
"The Plot Spread to Conecuh." Sept. 12, 1882.
"A Sad Case." Sept. 19, 1885.
"A Sad Case Denied." Sept. 20, 1885.
Sept. 18, 1868.
"Smith Revival Huge Success." Aug. 3, 1926.
"Ten Thousand Hear 'Gypsy Pat' Speak." Aug. 1, 1927.
"The Theatres." Sept. 27, 1896.
"The Wrong Gypsy." July 3, 1927.
"Union Springs." Sept. 23, 1885.

*Montgomery Times*
"Evangelist Gypsy Smith Objects To Use Name In Savannah Campaign." Dec. 11, 1922.
"Shocco Springs—Alabama's Ideal Summer Resort." May 21, 1925.

*New England Farmer* (Boston, MA)
May 16, 1857.

*New York Times*
"'Chief Architect' Of New Race Here." Aug. 28, 1907.

*North Alabamian* (Tuscumbia)
Rexford, Eben E. "The Swamp Secret—A Story of the Frontier (Chapter XVIII)." Jan. 19, 1900.

*Opelika Times*
Aug. 19, 1876.
"The Choctaw Conspiracy." Aug. 25, 1882.
George, William. "Camp Meeting In Little Texas." July 15, 1881.
"Letter From Tuskegee." Aug. 22, 1884.
"Our Correspondents—Our Auburn Items." Aug. 31, 1877.
"Uprising of Negroes Checked—One Negro Hung"; "Insurrection in Choctaw County Nipped in Nick of Time." Aug. 25, 1882.

*Pantagraph* (Bloomington, IL)
"A Colored Camp Meeting." Sept. 16, 1887.

*Pickens County Herald and West Alabamian* (Carrollton)
Ashcraft, Elder William. "Circular Letter." Nov. 20, 1867.
"The Camp Meeting at Unity Grove." Oct. 14, 1885.
"Unity Grove Camp Meeting." Oct. 21, 1885.

*Piedmont Inquirer*
July 9, 1892.

*Pittsfield Sun* (Pittsfield, MA)
"Avery's Trial." May 30, 1833.
"Camp Meeting." Sept. 9, 1830.
"Mr. Avery Acquitted." June 6, 1833; June 13, 1833.

*Record-Journal* (Meriden, CT)
"Darien Man Awarded Divorce From Gypsy Pat." July 23, 1928.

*Roanoke Leader*
"Editorial Tidbits." April 29, 1903.
"Sheriff Kent And His Duty." Sept. 9, 1903.
"The Star Rejoins." Sept. 16, 1903.
"The War Is Over." Sept. 23, 1903.

*Russell Register* (Seale)
"One Evangelist." Sept. 30, 1921.

*Rutland Weekly Herald* (Rutland, VT)
"Beating Fanaticism Out Of A Man." Oct. 8, 1846.

*Salem Herald-Advocate* (Salem, IL)
Oct. 7, 1887.

*Selma Morning Times*
April 14, 1870.

"The Choctaw Trouble." Sept. 17, 1882.
"Letter from Dundee." May 9, 1871.

*Selma Times-Journal*
Aug. 8, 1926.
"Camp Meeting." Sept. 15, 1882.
"City And County." Sept. 20, 1882.
"Great Crowds At Last Day Of Marengo Meet." July 27, 1925.
"Interesting Discussion on Camp Meetings." May 16, 1884.
"Large Crowds Hear Noted Evangelist At Dixon's Mills." Aug. 6, 1927.
Seay, C. C. "Bring Out Best In Nature, Plea Of Gypsy Smith." Nov. 21, 1929.
"Thomasville News." Aug. 7, 1927.

*Southern Republican* (Demopolis)
"General Correspondence." Dec. 28, 1870.

*Southern Star* (Ozark)
Parker, William D. "History of Ozark and Dale County." Oct. 26, 1939.
Sept. 30, 1885.

*St. Clair News Aegis* (Pell City)
Blair, Edmund. "W-A-K-E of the N-E-W-S." Aug. 13, 1953.

*Time* magazine
"Letters." July 16, 1928.
"Milestones." July 2, 1928.

*Times and News* (Eufaula)
Aug. 4, 1885.
Billings, Josh. Sept. 7, 1881.

*Times-Argus* (Selma)
"Big Camp-Meeting at Little Texas." Aug. 28, 1885.

*Trenton Evening News* (Trenton, NJ)
"To Bar Men From Trinity's Pulpit." Aug. 7, 1909.

*Tri-Weekly Nashville Union*
"Rev. E. K. Avery." Jan. 23, 1844.

*Troy Messenger*
"Gen. Jack Turner." Aug. 31, 1882.
July 28, 1887.
"Short Locals." Dec. 15, 1892.

*Tuscaloosa News*
"Communicated." July 1, 1927.
"'Gypsy' Pat Smith Divorce Is Served." July 22, 1927.

*Tuskegee News*
"The Camp Meeting." Aug. 30, 1877.
Samford, W. F. "The Old Camp-Meeting Days—William Arnold." (Wesleyan Christian Advocate). Oct. 9, 1884.

*Union-Banner* (Clanton)
"Alabama Woodmen Meeting to Be Held in Birmingham Soon." Mar. 9, 1933.
"Seventh-Day Adventists Hold Successful Meeting." Sept. 22, 1921.

*Union Springs Herald*
"The Camp Meeting." Sept. 22, 1880.
"Local Affairs." Sept. 25, 1889.
Sept. 7, 1881.

*Vermont Patriot and State Gazette* (Montpelier)
"Miscellany. The Case of Avery." Mar. 25, 1833.

*Weekly Advertiser* (Montgomery)
"Caption of Acts." Feb. 24, 1885.
"The Choctaw County Outragers." Oct. 7, 1874.
"Fatted Calf." Dec. 1, 1887.
Feb. 24, 1887.
"Fred Kidd Hung." Jan. 9, 1890.
"Hanging in Widowee." Oct. 2, 1903.
"Stevens Was Convicted." Aug. 28, 1903.

*Wilcox Progressive Era* (Camden)
Aug. 1, 1888.
Aug. 6, 1896.
"Aunt Tab's Letter." June 27, 1888.
"Bright Sparks From the [*indecipherable word*] Pen of Fair Mignonette." July 25, 1888.
"Editor Wilcox Progress." May 23, 1888.
July 8, 1896.
May 23, 1888.
"Mignonette's Warblings." Sept. 12, 1888.
"Our Circle." Apr. 10, 1889.
"The Pine Hill Barbecue." Aug. 19, 1909.
"The Rifles Picnic." May 8, 1889.

Sept. 12, 1888.
"Soldiers Dinner." Jan. 16, 1889.

*York Gazette* (PA)
"Another Strange Story." Jan. 16, 1844.

# Index

*Page numbers in italics refer to figures.*